When Zebras Discover Motorbikes

How to influence people, situations and results

Jonathan Frost

Copyright © 2015 Jonathan Frost

All rights reserved.

ISBN: 150887705X
ISBN-13: 978 - 1508877059

Published by Discovery Coaching Limited
Edinburgh

Cover: Mayfin Design

CONTENTS

About the Author

Introduction

PART 1
THE ZEBRA ANALOGY

1	The Zebra Analogy	3
2	'Natural Orders'	9
3	What made the difference?	17
4	The initial response - Denial	29
5	The second response - Work More, Work Harder	35
6	The third response - Redefine Success	43
7	The fourth response - Innovation	49

PART 2
5 STAGES OF CHANGE

8	Step 1 - Awareness	61
9	Step 2 - Engagement	73
10	Step 3 - Activity	79
11	Step 4 - Consistency	91
12	Step 5 - Continuous Improvement	97
13	Summary of Models and Techniques	109
	The Zebra Analogy II	117

ABOUT THE AUTHOR

Jonathan Frost is the Founder and Managing Director of Discovery Coaching Limited; a successful Coaching Consultancy based in Edinburgh, Scotland. Working across Europe he has assisted hundreds of managers and directors over the last 17 years clocking up thousands of hours of coaching experience.

He has a unique ability to provoke thought, trigger discoveries and reinforce learning. His focus is on enabling participants to discover practical tips, hints and techniques that are relevant to their everyday leadership life. Jonathan developed the coaching methodology known as 'Discovery Coaching' and this proven approach helps individuals to develop their leadership approach, maximize their performance and manage difficult situations. He is an inspirational coach who motivates leaders to excel.

Jonathan has extensive experience working with leaders at all levels in many different organisations; from small enterprises right through to large multinationals. This has included industries as diverse as retail, distribution, professional services, utilities, local government, defence and engineering.

Jonathan Frost

INTRODUCTION

This book is for those whose success depends on the activity, engagement and performance of others. It has been written primarily for those who have the responsibility to deliver organisational success and therefore need to influence people and situations. As a supervisor, manager, leader or key influencer you know that if you engage people to see things differently and do things differently, you will gain better results and everyone will have a better quality of working life. The book provides some practical tips and techniques that you will find useful to trigger such change in a way that is both helpful and long lasting.

It starts with a light-hearted parable I call 'The Zebra Analogy'. It talks about 'change' at work and draws your attention to some of the typical reactions that people have when faced with it; you are encouraged to think about your own personal 'patterns of behaviour' and typical responses. You will notice that the parable storyline is fairly 'tongue in cheek' and it is important not to focus on the practical realism of it, but rather on the bigger messages that it provides. Chapters 1 through to 7 digest the Zebra Analogy and extract helpful insights that you can personally apply in your working life. Chapter 8 onwards provides a 5-step process that you can use to trigger a change in the contribution and impact of those in your personal 'sphere of influence'. You might want to trigger change in you, your team or even your organisation; the model highlights the difference between awareness, engagement and activity.

At the end of each chapter you will notice that I have provided some 'thought provokers'. These are self-explanatory and are designed to trigger careful consideration about some of the points noted in the text; they are useful for you to ensure a personal engagement and to use as a helpful tool to engage your team in this thinking. I would strongly recommend that you don't gloss over the 'thought provokers'. If you look for more than superficial responses, you will discover helpful ways to impact your working world and be a positive influence.

PART 1

THE ZEBRA ANALOGY

Jonathan Frost

1

THE ZEBRA ANALOGY

It happened on a Thursday...

"On the plains of the Serengeti in Africa the sun comes up, the animals stir and little zebras stretch and yawn. Everyone starts preparing for the challenges of the day. They have to find good grazing spots and good water supplies. More importantly they have to be prepared to run...and run very fast.

They know that to survive they need to run faster than the fastest lion. This is because across the plains, the lions are also waking up and they are preparing for the challenges of their day. The lions know that if they are going to survive they have to run; at least to run faster than the slowest zebra. Whether you are a zebra or a lion it is guaranteed to be a challenging and active day. The lions tend to look forward to the running a little more than the zebras... 'The pursuit of gain' is always a lot more fun than the 'fleeing of pain!'

It was on a Thursday morning however that the 'natural

order' of things changed. The hunting party reported back to the King of the pride with no kills at all. The King roared his disapproval and asked for an explanation. "The zebras have discovered motorbikes" was the reply, "We could not catch them".

At first the lions carried on as normal; they acted as if nothing had changed. They eagerly hoped for the day that the zebras would not have this advantage, they waited patiently for the 'natural order' to be returned. The King grew angrier, the pride hungrier and the hunting pack more humiliated.

So the lions ran faster and faster. They organised extra hunting parties and threw every ounce of energy into the hunt. Their increased determination, fitness levels and extra activity certainly helped; however they were not feeding all of the pride all of the time. The King grew angrier, the pride remained hungry and the hunters remained humiliated.

The hunting party had a meeting with the King. In the light of developments and in recognition for their hard work and 'round the clock' hunting parties – they asked the King to change the 'daily zebra budget'. "We have to be realistic" they implored, "We are working harder, running faster and hunting around the clock…you cannot expect so much…things have changed!" In no uncertain terms the King refused their request. "If things have changed, then you had better change too!" he roared at them.

With the words of the King ringing in their furry ears the lions went away crestfallen. They discussed the situation at length. They pooled their ideas, identified some options and developed some different tactics. They stopped the fruitless chases across the plains. They stopped trying to outrun motorbikes. They started watching the behaviour of the zebras with a new intensity; they carefully considered what had actually changed and when the zebras might be just as vulnerable as they were before.

The lions blockaded petrol stations. The zebras lost their advantage and 'natural order' appears to have been restored."

Jonathan Frost

2

'NATURAL ORDERS'

As you read the story I am sure that like me, you would rather be the lion than the zebra. You seldom hear of a pack of zebras hunting down a lion, the threat does appear to be rather one sided. It is no coincidence that there is a well known saying about the 'lions share' i.e. in Aesop's fables when the lion goes hunting with a partner and it comes to the point of dividing the spoils, it all goes the lion's way. The 'lion's share' is the bigger portion of any deal and it reflects the seniority, authority and strength of the lion. If you were heading up the negotiation for a significant deal, you would not return to your office and proudly proclaim that you have secured the 'zebras share' of the profits!

In the animal kingdom on the plains of Africa the lions do tend to win. This is the 'natural order' and natural orders can be very important drivers and protectors of organised society; they provide comfort, confidence, security and your 'daily zebra'. There is a very good chance that the lions were not giving much thought to this concept and the benefits that they were getting from it. They probably had been seeing their seniority and authority as a bit of a 'given' i.e. they had the 'right' to expect things to be the way that they always were. As stated in the story, the running that the lions participated in was fun, they were engaged in the pursuit of gain and they were good at it.

It is a very risky practice to see advantage, superiority or success as a 'given'. The very things that create success and advantage are all about being alert, fully engaged and focused. When these attributes are muted, hindered or no longer valued then complacency or even arrogance can become the norm. It is not easy to notice change or adaptation if you keep looking at things the way you have always looked at things. Taking advantage of 'natural orders' and even trying to establish them is a wise thing to do; the problems arise however when they are perceived to be permanent because they never can be. Time spent looking for and identifying shifts in 'natural orders' is time well spent.

It should be noted of course that the zebras did not wake up that Thursday morning surprised that motorbikes had been delivered or that they had been trained how to use them during their sleep! This had taken time for an individual to have the idea, to develop it into a concept, to discuss it with the group and to develop plans. It had taken time, focus and energy to make the contacts, set up the arrangements and commence training. Why did the lions not notice anything? Why had they been unaware of the changes in structure, outlooks and activities of the zebras?

Are you constructing your 'worldview' or just reinforcing it?

I wonder if the lions had become too reliant on the natural order of things and had begun to see it as their ongoing right rather than a current opportunity. Perhaps they had seen their superiority as a 'given' and were not looking out for any changes, threats or further opportunities. They may have unwittingly put themselves in a position in which they only noticed things that reinforced and confirmed their 'worldview', not the things that should have actually been developing and constructing it. We have all developed a view of our world around us so that we can make sense of it, see things in context and even predict what might be. This becomes our model of reality and it obviously influences our ideas, attitudes and activities. This can be a conscious state in which we are aware of it and think about it. This is helpful because it enables us to convert day-to-day work into a learning experience and this assists our progress and development. It works this way because we question things that don't seem to resonate with our worldview and we discover better ways to see things and different responses to them. You can trigger this thinking by simply asking yourself 'why' as much as possible.

Why do you *see* it that way?

Why did you *assume* that this would happen?

Why do you *prefer* this approach to a different one?

This understanding of your perspective, your assumptions and your preferences really stimulates self-development; it enables you to be open to new learning and add to your capability toolset.

It is also possible to be unaware of your own worldview simply because you do not think about it and therefore you are not actively engaged in understanding, changing or developing it. You will tend to see situations and results through the established prism and notice reasons to support and reinforce it. In the story we see that zebras were fundamental to the wellbeing of the lions and yet it is possible that this had been forgotten; it was not a pillar of their worldview. Perhaps they were only seeing them one dimensionally i.e. as readily available food. Had they understood how the zebras themselves were seeing the situation then they might have noticed things that would trigger their curiosity and lead to insight. It is very easy to see things but not actually notice them. How often have you driven to work, felt as if you were on automatic pilot, and you cannot remember anything about your journey? In fact you saw every junction, traffic sign and car in front of you, you simply did not notice (take note of) them. The lions might have noticed the new values that had emerged if they had been looking for change. If they had been questioning their 'world' and how things were working in the Serengeti they might have noticed the improved teamwork of the zebras. Perhaps had they focused on zebra tactics, the lions might have noticed the extra hard work and their determination to succeed? Had they understood the aspirations of the zebras then they would have suspected that they were looking for a radical approach. This understanding of the psychological drivers of the Zebras would have triggered an awareness and recognition of the behaviours and actions that would have supported them. If you have been told that someone is very quick to take offence, you are very conscious about the words you use and you look for signs that they have been misinterpreted. In the same way if the lions had been thinking about the aspirations of the zebras they would have noticed the new behaviours and activities. That is why the story ended with the natural order only 'apparently' being restored; those factors that inspired the zebras to change have not gone away.

Whilst we are looking at the culture of the zebras we should also look at the attitudes and customs of the lions. I wonder if 'passive acceptance' was valued more highly than 'active curiosity'? It would appear that none of the senior lions were engaged in questioning life in the Serengeti. The senior lions were reinforcing the apparent stability of the natural order of things and it is easy to see why. Driving, leading, managing and supervising change is a fundamental role of leadership and the senior lions should have been taking the lead in this. Perhaps some junior lions had noticed strange happenings but they knew that such information would not be welcomed or even ridiculed. The zebras were celebrating curiosity and different ways of seeing things; the lions were celebrating consistency and stability.

Whilst it is nice to be benefitting from a 'natural order' I would strongly suggest that you question whether any sort of order is natural at all. The word 'natural' suggests that it is derived from something bigger than mankind i.e. from nature. We often link the word natural to being supremely right and obviously best. If something is natural then it is not questioned, after all, 'Who are we to question nature?' This is an important distinction; if we see structures, processes, authorities and values as being 'natural' then we do not question them. They become established as a part of our worldview and we do not question, look for ways to improve or to add value to them.

Beware of 'self-imposed limitations'

If we simply accept that our situations and circumstances are 'naturally right' then we develop a comforting, but very unhelpful, illusion of stability. Such an illusion can develop into a self-imposed limitation. This is a very important principle; allow me to explain. Large trucks or buses often have a 'limiter' fitted and this prevents the vehicle exceeding a certain speed. It does not matter how much you stamp on the accelerator or shift the gears it is unable to go faster than a defined speed; the speed is limited.

As supervisors, managers, leaders and key influencers we can also have 'limiters' that hinder our ability to progress at speed. These might be our levels of authority, our access to resources, our available time or even our limited capability; they limit us because if things were different we would get better results. A self-imposed limitation occurs when we have thoughts, activities or outlooks that are both optional and unhelpful. It is the optional element that makes them self-imposed i.e. we might choose to carry emotional 'baggage' that we do not need to. When confronted with realities we may choose to deny them. We may make things more complicated than they need to be or reframe situations so that they are more convenient; these will indeed limit our success. If we choose not to question our circumstances and reframe *'current stability'* as a *'right'* for things to be stable (as did the lions) then we have introduced a significant self-imposed limitation. Such an error would stop us looking for change and this in turn would stop us from noticing it. In today's world of fast changing technology, geography, morals, knowledge and cultures – can anything in your organisational life be considered as a 'given' or the 'natural order'?

Rather than the above being a sobering thought I would like to suggest that it is a liberating one. It shows that change is good and that you can use your creativity, enthusiasm, innovation and flexibility to trigger helpful changes; these in turn can give you a competitive advantage. For the zebras of the workplace you can innovate, change and discover motorbikes. For the lions it means you too can innovate and change - you can gain even more advantage.

Useful 'thought-provokers' for zebras and lions

Would your team feel like the lions or the zebras in this story? Are they fighting to preserve a comfortable status quo or are they engaged in improvement? What is the underlying 'driver' for your team? What is inspiring or triggering focus and activity?

Do you see areas of complacency in your sphere of influence? Are people basking in the sunshine of an assumed 'natural order advantage'? Do they know it?

In your team is there a helpful balance between maintaining stability and triggering consistent change? How do you know the balance is right? What would be the 'indicators' of a good balance?

Are you able to see the key influencers within your working world in more than one dimension? Remember how the lions only saw the zebras through the filter of 'food'…they did not see the creativity, innovation, determination or drive.

Who are the winners in the story? Hopefully this is a bit of a difficult question and it probably depends on what time frame you choose. Which team is in the pursuit of 'winning' as opposed to being in the pursuit of 'not losing'?

Are you continuously constructing your world-view or simply reinforcing it? Your outlook, understanding and sense of context should always be 'work in progress'. There are a multitude of factors influencing your personal situation and sphere of influence – many of which you have no control over. This triggers a need for you to be alert to change and have the agility to respond to it.

Can you list any 'self-imposed limitations' for your team? These can be…
Limiting beliefs
Unhelpful attitudes
Inappropriate outlooks
Unwise use of resources
Compromised positions
Lack of capabilities

3

WHAT MADE THE DIFFERENCE?

What made the difference for the zebras? When I have asked this question in workshops most people immediately answer 'technology' i.e. the motorbikes. It is true to say that the machinery gave them a speed, reliability and an endurance advantage; however if you think a little deeper, the motorbikes are probably more of a *result* of the change than actually being the cause of it. Some might say that it was teamwork that enabled a new 'order' to be introduced because the zebras had to think and work together to hatch their cunning plan. Again I can see the logic of this but what provoked the teamwork? There is seldom a sudden and unexpected outbreak of collaboration and teamwork in organisations; something triggers it and then it develops. It is probably more relevant to say that *somebody* as opposed to something triggers it.

Can you have good vision with poor eyesight?

The answer is a definite 'Yes'! Obviously this is a play on words and it reveals an important business lesson; *Eyesight can see 'what is'…Vision can see 'what could be'*. This is an important distinction for both the lions and the zebras. The lions were comfortable and were seeing 'what is'; and because they liked it they were not driven to see it differently. The zebras were uncomfortable with the status quo and so they were

looking at 'what could be'; this resulted in a change of vision. The two key triggers for change amongst the zebras were…
>Vision
>Meaningful Communication.

At least one of the zebras had to be able to picture, in his minds eye, just how different things could and should be. He had to understand and harness the herd's drive and determination to change the 'natural order' of the lions. He had to take a simple *thought* and develop it into an *idea* that could be shared and meaningfully communicated. For me there is a difference between a thought and an idea and it is all about application. A thought can just occur whereas an idea is formed. It is formed when you work on the thought, think about how to apply it, link it to other things and make it work for you. It is very easy to just think about things without going on to generate ideas about how to helpfully apply them. We can see this in people when they think *about* issues without thinking them *through*.

The next step was for that idea to be converted into a *concept*. It is not enough to have bright ideas and momentary flashes of inspiration, these need to be crafted into a coherent proposition that is both understandable and practical i.e. a concept. That concept, once discussed and approved with your key stakeholders, can then be developed into a *plan*. This is what a true vision is all about; it is the outcome of an idea being worked on until you can actually 'see' (visualise) it in your minds eye. It is hard but rewarding work and is a key part of leadership. Do not confuse this type of visionary thinking with the huge 'visionaries' such as Henry Ford, Andrew Carnegie, Thomas Edison or Steve Jobs. *Developing a vision is not the same as being a Visionary.* Few in this world are genuine visionaries; however all of us in leadership positions need to be able to develop a vision of what 'could be' and 'what we would like to be' in our working worlds. We then convert this vision into a cunning plan.

Thought…Idea…Concept…Plan

It is often said, *"He who has the vision, has the job"*. This points to the fact that the person with the vision has to exert energy, influence and wisdom to drive it until it has enough momentum of its own to make significant progress. In the real world of work there are very few people who can get away with being just 'an ideas person', someone who is only responsible for thinking up weird and wonderful ideas. Creative thinking and innovative tactics are the responsibility of all leaders and managers; this activity is not reserved for a few individuals. That zany zebra with a big vision, who was mentioned earlier, had to have some insight and clarity about the different ways that it could be achieved and he had to see the necessary and sequential steps that it would take to bring it to fruition. He then had to make others aware of it and engage them in the process. He had to 'drive' things so that progress could be made. This is a tall order for a zebra but in the real world it's what 'purpose-driven' leaders do all the time. They see situations, opportunities and processes that could be improved; they generate ideas; these are developed into carefully considered concepts; they are then discussed and developed into plans.

It is my experience that people hold onto their ideas, concepts and visions too long because they think that they are not good enough or because they want to 'smooth out the rough edges' before presenting them to the team. This is not helpful and is usually counterproductive. Situations and circumstances change quickly and it is a never-ending process of 'catch-up' if you are trying to wait for perfection. A 75% worked through vision is always better than no vision!

This is where 'meaningful communication' becomes so important. The leadership population have to ensure that the key stakeholders…

Grasp the Concept
Own the Journey
Personally Make a Difference.

When a good number of people have a common vision and a common strategy they start working together; they combine their energy, focus and capability into achieving this goal. This creates an added value and strength that can achieve great things. It is important to recognise whether the vision is owned and pursued by one person or by the whole leadership team? I often hear teams talking about 'Andy's vision' when they really should be talking about 'our' vision or at least 'the' vision. With ownership comes responsibility and accountability and in working life these are essential success factors. You cannot be an observer of your own journey, you have to be fully engaged and a key player in it.

The football analogy

When talking about ownership and engagement I like to use the football analogy. There are at least 5 key stakeholders in the game including spectators, pundits, players, the captain and the manager. It is very helpful to identify who, in your sphere of influence, is playing which role.

Spectators are fully engaged in the game and they can have a fierce passion and loyalty that is admirable. They personally live every play of the ball and scream and shout encouragement or derision at the players. They are fully immersed in the state of play and desperately wish for success. It must be noted however that on an individual basis they have absolutely no influence on the result. Even working together as a huge collective, with all their singing and shouting, they can only have a small effect. You want to watch out for the spectators on your team, the people who make a noise but don't make a difference. Their emotional engagement is real and their passion is obvious but they simply don't have a practical contribution to make. They might be proud of their 'supporting role' however this should not be confused with the value of a 'contributing role'. It is great to support…it's not enough to only support.

Pundits might be helpful to remote spectators (watching on television) but they have no influence on the game. They analyse every move and situation with great observations about what is happening and what should be happening. Most times they do not have the level of passion that the spectators have, they are just doing their job. They are not responsible for the success of the team in any way and are often required to hide their team preferences. Pundits have no influence at all on the result. *Beware of the pundits in your organisation that masquerade as involved players or managers.* They might comment from the safety of the press box and have flowing opinions about what could have happened, should have happened or might have happened. They don't have any involvement in or responsibility for the team's success but they can divert focus, draw attention and even create work.

Players obviously make a direct difference because their outlooks, approaches and activities create winning opportunities. As a leader it is obviously important not to unconsciously assume the position of a spectator or pundit; in the same way however you do not want to be just a player.

Captains are on the pitch and are 'on site' leaders. Captains have a significant influence because of the application of their personal skills in the game as well as their leadership of the team. Usually this position is given as a result of their experience, respect from the team and their ability to 'read' the game. This role is helpful in implementing the pre-planned tactics and bringing a discipline to the players. It is obviously a leadership role but is it the right role for you in your position? Should you be in the thick of it, exercising 'in the moment' leadership or should you be standing back considering tactics and strategies? It is a genuine question (not a leading question) because different roles and circumstances require different approaches. It is essential however that this is a conscious decision. As the captain you don't get to choose the squad.

Managers influence the success of the team by shouting instructions and advice from the side as well as giving the half-time coaching talk. They are also influential through their role in developing the tactics and strategies for the team as well as the selection of the squad. It is important for you to be fully aware of your role in choosing the resources you want to employ and the tactics that the team must follow. If a manager is needed but you are operating as a captain you will create a leadership void; the team will rely on extra hard work, opportunism and individual brilliance to succeed as opposed to wise tactics and teamwork. If the team needs a captain and you are operating as a manager then a different type of leadership void will exist; discipline, coordination and teamwork will suffer so that the plans cannot be well implemented.

Different thinking can be a 'game changer'

We all know that it is impossible for zebras to start riding motorbikes, however if they were able to think differently, to communicate better and to organise themselves better…they would beat the lions! If they used their strengths and resources wisely they could permanently change the natural order that the lions enjoy. Imagine if our zebra with the ideas had another one which went along the lines of *"…every single time we see a lion…we will all stampede towards it at full speed and trample it to death"* – it could lead to interesting times in the Serengeti.

As long as the herd a) grasped the concept, b) each owned the responsibility for stampeding and c) decided to personally make a difference to the fierceness of the stampede – it would be a game changer for both the lions and the zebras! It would shift the risk of a zebra-lion encounter over to the lions; it would be *their* risk. They might even start avoiding zebras! Even with all their fierce roaring and mighty strength a few lions could not cope with fifty zebras stampeding at them; very quickly they would see zebras as a high-risk threat rather than high calorie meal. This is how having a vision and some meaningful collaboration can make all the difference.

The zebras could, if they had a strong enough vision and a good enough communication capability, adopt a different strategy of what to do when approached by a lion. Imagine if they formed a tight circle, like wheel spokes, all with their noses in the middle and as soon as a lion approached they told each other when to kick viciously. The lions would start getting severely injured. Again they would fear an encounter with the zebras and go instead for easier targets. If zebras do what zebras have always done then they will be subject to the challenges that they have always had. If they see things differently, feel differently about things and make different decisions, then things will change. If they employ different tactics and engage in close teamwork they would get very different results. This perfectly reflects the real world of influential management in your workplace.

True leadership involves taking the responsibility for creating and maintaining an environment where people have common goals, aligned outlooks and coordinated activities; it is not enough to just have a 'common goal'. Currently when the zebras are fleeing the lions and are running for their lives they certainly have a common goal (to escape the lions) but this is not enough to enable smart tactics or approaches.

They are operating as individuals rather than as a team because they are not supporting or assisting each other. They cannot be considered a team because they are not collaborating, encouraging and enabling each other to achieve the goal; this can have very severe consequences. The valid and common intention at individual level triggers zebras to do whatever they personally can to escape the danger; this can lead to conflicts, confusion and the undermining of each other. Inadvertently they get in each other's way, trip each other and expose the herd to risk. This uncoordinated approach (with a common purpose) can rapidly degenerate even further; it can quickly involve the leap from *'not working together'*…to become *'working against each other'!* This happens when the goal changes because individuals become aware that they don't actually have to run faster than the fastest lion…*they just have to run faster than the slowest zebra!*

Even this can degenerate further; they realise the value of positioning smaller and slower zebras between them and the lions as this makes their personal survival much more likely. In this case exactly the opposite of what I suggested earlier happens; instead of the zebras gaining collective strength and power they actually lose the value of collectiveness because it is every zebra for himself!

This happens in organisations in which divisions or teams have to compete aggressively with others to secure resources, budgets or opportunities. It can be seen when one part of a company has a ring fenced and strongly protected surplus whilst another withers and shrinks because it cannot get access to funds. I have seen it happen in sales organisations when two people from the same business are competing with each other to sell to the same customer, they start undercutting the other and offering more incentives in order to win. I have personally experienced two retail branches of the same company honouring the promise to beat any price and engaging each other in an aggressive price war! It also happens when one part of the business is on a mission to cut costs, increase margin and drive efficiency, whilst the other side is tasked with quickly growing market share and expanding. When an organisation has to compete internally as well as externally with its competitors, it is weakened and the people within it become demoralised.

So we see that a lack of vision and meaningful communication not only stops good things from happening, it can actually make bad things happen! Obviously this is all just a parable…but the principles it outlines are valid for you, your team and your workplace.

Useful 'thought-provokers' about connections

Are your people linked by a common situation or a common goal? There is a big difference between a common experience and a common determination. The first one provides a feeling of togetherness, identity and camaraderie and this can be useful for helping people to relate better and communicate more helpfully. The second one also provides these feelings but in addition it generates more focus and an awareness of the interdependencies needed to succeed.

Who holds the vision? In your team, division or organisation is the vision owned and pursued by one person or by the whole leadership team?

Is communication and collaboration a strength for your team? For a team or organisation to be 'in the know' it needs to gather and share information and insight. It also needs to have the mechanisms that make this easy and natural. Such mechanisms include briefings, meetings, reports, discussions, 1:1 meetings, workshops and even 'offsites'. For a team to use this insight to develop wise plans and tactics it needs to develop ideas, discuss them, deliberate over options and come to an agreement over the way forward. Without this you simply have people working independently as opposed to interdependently. Meaningful communication is required for this and people have to be in a 'state' of relationship for this to happen well. The analogy that I would use to elaborate on the 'state of relationship' is that of a wifi network. It is connected all the time, everybody can send and receive at will and the message, image or data is almost instantaneously delivered; this is a true state of connectedness and should be the goal. It demands both formal and informal communication practices in the workplace and structured meetings will help but so will informal conversations, chance gatherings at the coffee machine, shared jokes and telephone chats. The more that you can get your team to talk and engage then the quicker and smarter their teamwork will be. It is no use having an outstanding corporate strategy if nobody sees it or acts on it.

Does your organisational culture value and reward outstanding individual performance or outstanding teamwork? The quick answer to this question is normally 'both' however if you look closely there is bound to be a preference. If the preference appears to be for high performing individuals you should carefully evaluate the impact it is having, it could be hindering teamwork.

In your organisation how do people treat the slower zebras, the younger ones or those less capable? Carefully considering this question is valuable because it gives you an insight into the levels of teamwork, common purpose and maturity of the team.

4

THE INITIAL RESPONSE - DENIAL

…At first the lions carried on as normal – they acted as if nothing had changed. They eagerly hoped for the day that the zebras would not have this advantage, they waited patiently for the 'natural order' to be returned. The King grew angrier, the pride hungrier and the hunting pack more humiliated.

It is interesting to look at the initial response of the lions. As an experienced Executive Coach and Consultant of many years, it is my observation that 'carrying on as normal' in the face of significant change is typical workplace behaviour.

It can rightly be argued that it is not wise to react massively to everything that happens and that it might be very appropriate to 'sit tight' and let things play out their natural course of events. In this case however it became quite clear that this was not a 'self healing' problem for the lions. I don't see them engaged in admirable perseverance. Perseverance in the face of challenges and difficulties builds character and in the long run it is a helpful and enabling experience; it is a positive development that should be encouraged and rewarded. What the lions exhibited however was more a case of denial and avoidance rather than perseverance. Sometimes this is presented as 'patience' and it could well be. You do not always know at the time whether you are displaying considered patience or irritating procrastination…there has to come a time however when you must make the choice and consciously state it is either one or the other. It would certainly appear that the lions crossed over from patience into procrastination in a big way.

It is always wise to frequently ask yourself the question, "Are things changing?" This change could be about people, relationships or situations. It might point to significant changes in the working environment or company values. Sometimes change can be subtle and individuals may simply not notice that things have become significantly different. As human beings we have an amazing ability to cope with things and quietly adapt to situations, this can work for us but it can also work against us. There are times when we get used to challenges and problems and we develop coping mechanisms rather than taking positive actions to remedy it. We can even take pride in our ability to 'keep standing' despite all of the terrible things that happen to us. This is admirable and inspiring if you are in a position in which you cannot influence the hardship; it is just plain silly if you have the ability to change things but rather spend time coping. If you are shipwrecked on a deserted island and you make a shelter for yourself and manage to survive a major storm, you are a hero. If you are in your garden and make a shelter against the major storm and risk your life, instead of going inside, then you are an idiot. The difference is all about the reasoning behind the choices that are made.

Sometimes a failure to respond to change is a

matter of not linking all the pieces of the jigsaw together so that the need to, or opportunity to, is simply not seen. Individuals may understand each select piece of information but do not link them to see an overall picture, trend or shift. This is like trying to do a jigsaw without having a photo of what the finished product will look like. It is possible, but it is certainly a much more difficult task and it would involve identifying segments that obviously link and then trying to join them together. This means collecting all the straight edges together, the blue-sky pieces together, the different blue water pieces etc. After a while, parts of the picture emerge and you can interpret what it should be. However it is very easy to get distracted whilst this is going on because you see activity but you do not see much meaningful progress; the 'direct causal link' between activity and success is not seen clearly. This often means that attention and focus is lost or it becomes firmly attached to a part of the process and not to the whole process. This can result in an activity becoming the goal rather than simply being a step towards achieving the goal.

It is my experience that it is much easier to spot change if you are consistently looking for it. If you are alert to the symptoms, the triggers, the evidence, the shifts, the trends…then you will notice them. If you are not looking for these things then you will not notice them and you will not respond until such times as the effects are so large that they demand and get your attention. This can be costly and those who are more attuned will have an advantage over you. Initially the lions were not looking for opportunities to change and so they did not see any.

Another worrying reason for not recognising and responding to change is a 'denial' of the whole situation. This is a sophisticated version of the monkey covering his eyes and feeling comforted that the danger is not there, because he cannot see it. In this sense the denial is not a considered response; it is just a simplistic rejection. It is removing the issue from your consciousness so that, to you, it does not exist anymore. This is a very risky strategy for a manager or leader to adopt. The perception of wellbeing amongst the lions was a false one and did not represent their reality at all. It would have had very serious consequences had the King not intervened.

When people are in denial they can be surprisingly creative in the ways that they 're-frame' the situation to justify their position. We all know it can be relatively easy to manipulate statistics to prove a point. This 'creative avoidance' can have a stalling effect on wise and appropriate responses and it can create uncertainty and confusion. Often it erodes respect for those in leadership and this can be far-reaching and hard to win back. It can also cause concern that 'management are not telling us things' because a feeling emerges that 'they' are obviously ignoring a situation that requires a leadership response. An additional hindrance is that those in the organisation that do see the need and opportunity to change have to expend much of their energy, enthusiasm and time convincing others. They spend time persuading people, gathering data and winning groups over rather than engaging in forward looking helpful activities.

Perhaps the most worrying reason of all about not responding to change is seeing it clearly but not knowing what to do. It is certainly not a weakness to admit that you don't know what to do, but it is if you stay that way! If you are not responding to or reacting to change because you have made a conscious, thought-through decision to 'weather the storm'…this is called strategy and is a matter of leadership judgment. It is usually founded on experience, insight, advice or calculation; if this is not the case it might be denial. You might be avoiding a difficult decision or don't see the need when everyone else does; that represents a leadership void.

'What is the difference between perseverance and stubbornness?' I would answer with one word – wisdom. Such wisdom comes from proactively looking for change and recognising both the causes and effects of it. It results from linking perspectives, data and observations together and then taking a multidimensional view. This wisdom comes from searching for and being able to find 'direct causal links' between what people are doing and the success that they are having. It takes effort, focus, time and determination to engage in such wise thinking and it needs to be a conscious and determined approach. Effective leaders value it highly enough to engage with it.

Useful 'thought-provokers' for you in your leadership role

Are you alert to changes in your working environment? Are there any significant changes in outlooks, activities, approaches and environments that impact you? Do you have early warning metrics that act like a red flashing dashboard light?

Do you see situations in your work place in which people are persevering rather than innovating? Are some people making heroes out of themselves for coping with problems and challenges rather than fixing them? Does your leadership style reinforce or even create this unhelpful situation?

Do you have the mechanisms and organisational structure to make sure that people see the bigger picture? Is it down to individuals to notice things or are there meetings, announcements, briefings and other forms of communication to ensure that everybody is appropriately 'in the know'? It is my observation that in the absence of good information, people simply make things up (based on inferences, assumptions and chatter) and this can be very unhelpful; after a while this perception becomes an accepted reality.

5

THE SECOND RESPONSE - WORK MORE, WORK HARDER.

...The lions ran faster and faster. They organised extra hunting parties and threw every ounce of energy into the hunt. Their increased determination, fitness levels and extra activity certainly helped...however they were not feeding all of the pride all of the time. The King grew angrier, the pride remained hungry and the hunters remained humiliated.

The lions recognised that waiting for things to change was not an appropriate strategy (because it was not working) and so they went on to another very common response – they increased their work rate. The lions ran faster, worked harder and implemented around the clock hunting parties. To me this shows that the lions had fully accepted that they were wrong to wait for the problem to pass and that they recognised the need to intervene and do things differently. It certainly points to a better degree of collaboration and teamwork and shows them being much more organised. They had to interact helpfully to discuss arrangements, divide duties and work out how best to 'staff up' to accommodate the new routines. It is of course very appropriate in the workplace to apply extra work and effort in response to challenges; this can have a positive effect of driving out inefficiencies, making processes leaner, increasing capability and even increasing 'hunger' for success. There are however a number of 'risks' that need to be managed when using this approach.

The risks of a 'work more, work harder' strategy…
- Treating symptoms and not root causes
- Extra becomes the 'new norm'
- Focus shifts from winning to coping
- Creation of leadership voids
- 'One level down' working

If a doctor only treated the symptoms of an ailment of yours, you might actually feel better and think that progress is being made with your healing; when in fact nothing is really being done to address the root cause of it. This applies in the workplace as well because it can be *easier and quicker* to throw extra resources and effort at a problem rather than carefully understanding the situation and looking for its root causes. Extra hunting parties and super fit lions are a visible response to the problem and this will give the Pride reassurance and comfort because somebody is obviously doing something about the difficulty. It would appear that this approach did get some improvement and again this would have been encouraging for those who were suffering. It has been my observation that an increased work rate with increased efficiency and extra hours can indeed solve the apparent problems and help the organisation over the short term. It is also my experience however that long hours, highly developed fire fighting expertise and corner cutting can mean that the real issues and challenges of the business are hidden because teams and individuals learn to cope; senior leaders see no reduction in performance. This creates a comfortable ignorance about just how hard it is to deliver the basics and I call this the 'illusion of ability'. The illusion is that the company can thrive in this situation when in actual fact it is only able to cope. Once again it means that managers and leaders are seen as remote and out of touch and this negatively impacts on their influence and authority.

A linked risk that has to be managed when using this approach is that the extra work and effort can very quickly become the new 'norm' in the organisation rather than a temporary response. Suddenly the extra hours become the standard hours and the extra hunting parties become the usual number of hunting parties; everyone is stretched without any recognition of it in terms of understanding, budgets or remuneration. I see this in organisations where people come in early or stay late all the time and even seem to appreciate the 'after hours' time in the office because it is quieter and they can get more work done. Others take work home with them and to achieve a sense of 'being in control' they put in a few hours later that night. This 'after hours' element of work that is all about keeping your head above water is actually contributing to the problem. The fact that it is not seen or measured means that more and more work is created and expected because it all seems to be coped with during the visible working day.

It is blindingly obvious that this is an unhelpful situation and that it has ongoing ramifications in terms of morale, goodwill and work quality. It also means that there is no slack in the system for when new opportunities or challenges arise. I have seen some organisations that operate this way be absolutely astounded to discover that their employees (managers included) *don't* want to win any more business! The team actually hope that new pursuits are not successful because they are totally stretched and do not believe that they can deliver any more. This is a terrible position to be in because your management team may become blockers of change or development. This happens because more work, for resources that are already stretched, creates a direct threat to how their performance is perceived. This then has a knock-on effect as some of the experienced 'corner stones' leave and get replaced by people without the same insight or experience; this then draws more and more time and energy from the management population.

There is another risk created by this unplanned *'work more and work harder'* approach; the focus of the organisation can begin to subtly shift away from its original strategy and tactics; it becomes adept at winning *despite* the circumstances, structure and resources, not because of them. All focus is on coping with the present and whilst this works for a while, it is unsustainable and in the long run it creates further challenges and problems. Consider the lions, no matter how fast they ran or how fit they became, they were never going to outrun a motorbike. Over time they would have worked harder and harder and become more and more exhausted…until their performance started obviously deteriorating. In the throes of exhaustion simple tasks become difficult and you get diminishing returns on the energy that you expend. If you have ever wondered why there are no 5000m sprints in the Olympics it is for this very reason – nobody can sprint for 5000m! You have a very different race strategy for a 400m race than you do for a 5000m event; in one you set off at a fast pace and use up all of your energy in under a minute and in the other you use appropriate amounts of energy spreading it over 12-14 minutes. If you get these two strategies confused you have big problems and so it is in the work place.

The fourth risk of this approach is that the role and contribution of the key influencers in the organisation starts to change. Leaders and managers take up some of the work and activities of their teams to help out and they shift closer to the front line as opposed to standing back and seeing the bigger picture. They become a very expensive 'extra pair of hands' and this creates a leadership void; whilst they are doing someone else's job, nobody is doing theirs.

This can then provoke senior leaders to get involved to 'help out' and this can create different problems all of its own. The senior managers are influenced by what they see and hear and become more involved using their insight and authority to provide fixes and unblock the blockages. This actually diminishes the influence of line managers, team leaders and supervisors because there is someone more senior involved; they are making decisions and taking authority. In the long run there is a real risk that everyone operates at 'one level down' and the organisation ends up being *over-managed* and *under-led*. You see this when the Operations Director acts like a Regional Manager, so the Regional Manager acts more like a Branch Manager, who responds to this by acting more like a Sales Manager, who in turn acts like a Sales Executive – I am sure that you see where this is going; in the long run nobody is actually doing the full management job that they are supposed to be doing.

Whilst the work rate and effort of the lions was commendable, it was not enough to actually solve the problem or even cope with it. There are times when difficulties and challenges need *inspiration* rather that *perspiration* and this certainly applied in this situation. Perspiration is all about the 'work more, work harder' approach in which greater effort and energy is demanded so that the team can get more done with the same resources. The Inspiration approach is all about doing things differently and doing different things. It includes being innovative, creative and open minded so that better ways can be identified. I would suggest that such thinking should be a regular agenda for leadership team offsites so that you can be ahead of the change and not always reacting to it.

As mentioned earlier our ability to cope with difficulties and amend our expectations to accommodate them can be a real hindrance when we want to move forward and make significant progress. Something is needed to trigger new thinking or a different understanding so that this in turn can trigger different activities. This requires leaders to take a wider perspective and to look at the macro picture; simply making people consistently work harder, work longer and fight fires all day is counter productive if the challenge is not a temporary one. This is why it is important for leaders to be able to step back and step up above the situation and to look at the business from a helpful altitude.

Useful 'thought-provokers' for your leadership role

Is there a 'long hours' culture in your organisation? Is it because people are working together, engaged in the pursuit of outstanding success so they choose to not be hindered by the clock…or is it because the workload cannot be done in a typical day?

How full is the 'Goodwill Tank' in your organisation? If morale, loyalty and goodwill were a balance sheet item, would they be listed under assets or liabilities? Are you running on empty or do you have reserves that can be used to help you take full advantage of new opportunities?

Are your managers 'doing' the business or 'leading' the business? Sometimes when times are hard and budgets are cut organisations revert to cutting back hours and relying on managers who are on salaries to take up the strain so that they do not incur overtime costs. This means that things are getting done, but the business is not developing, growing or being strengthened.

Is more perspiration or inspiration required from your team? Do you need people to exert more energy and work harder than they have before? Are you needing a higher work rate from individuals because there is slack in the way that resources are used? Alternatively, do you need the team to be more cunning, creative and innovative so that challenges can be overcome and opportunities taken advantage of? Do you need new ways of doing things to gain efficiency and productivity gains? As per the 400m and 5000m races – there is a different strategy needed for each. Whilst you are basically doing the same thing i.e. running a race – the way that you do it is very important. To stick with the sporting analogies, consider the professional golfer. She sets out with a golf bag that has a variety of clubs in it. She uses the driver if she needs to gain distance and the putter for precision shots. Mix these up and you have problems with your game; different tactics are needed for different situations. Your team need to know whether they should be working harder or working smarter.

6

THE THIRD RESPONSE - REDEFINE SUCCESS

...The hunting party had a meeting with the King. In the light of developments and in recognition for their hard work and 'round the clock' hunting parties – they asked the King to change the 'daily zebra budget'. "We have to be realistic" they implored, "We are working harder, running faster and hunting around the clock...you cannot expect so much...things have changed!" In no uncertain terms the King refused their request. "If things have changed, then you had better change too!" he roared at them.

The third response from the lions in our story relates to their attempt to change the 'indicators of success'; they asked the King to change the zebra budget. Again this is an area that requires wisdom.

To make people aim for a goal that cannot actually be achieved is both unreasonable and silly. It is unfair to hold people accountable for something that they cannot achieve because it sets them up for failure. On the other hand *changing targets to accommodate performance...rather than changing performance to accommodate targets* is also not the right thing to do. I am often surprised at managers and leaders who see targets and budgets as some sort of idealistic guideline that would be nice to achieve if you can. Significant business decisions are made in accordance with expected revenues and expenditures and when these differ from the forecast or plan it has a knock-on effect that impacts many areas. I must confess that I agree with the 'King' on this one; the zebra budget could not simply be changed to accommodate the current difficulties. This is a leadership issue more than it is an accounting issue. In this case many were relying on the 'zebra budget' and the consequences of not meeting it were very severe for the organisation.

Had the lions presented a case for a budget amendment based on current performance and all the different tactics that had been considered and tried, it might have been different. Essentially all that the lions had done up to this point is everything they had always done i.e. run after the zebras to catch them. To change requirements based on such standard tactics and the absence of real innovation would have been poor leadership. It would have signaled to all that it is acceptable to just change the goal when things get tough rather than changing behaviours or tactics.

Another reason that it would have been poor leadership is because it would have been a strategic error to signal defeat to the whole animal kingdom. It would have shown weakness to all the enemies of the lions and their Pride would have become vulnerable to attack. It would have been a very low blow to the group morale. It was also a matter of survival and a decision to change the zebra budget would have consigned some in the Pride to death because the current activities were simply not providing enough food for all. The fourth reason it would have been poor leadership is all to do with morale, it would have defeated the hard working lions in the pride. It may have been much easier, empathetic and understanding of the King to change the budget but it would not, in this instance, have been good leadership.

The lions had not *responded* to the situation they found themselves in; they had merely *reacted* to it. The difference between these two is all about depth of thought and a real understanding of the goals that they were working to. As I read the story I saw the goal of the lions shift from one of 'gathering food for all' to become one of 'avoiding the wrath of the King' and it was this subtle but very dangerous shift that was so destructive and unhelpful. It meant that the hunting parties could create a context that would enable them to think it was reasonable for some in the Pride to starve. Perhaps only the King had noticed it. *Their goal had changed and this meant that their outlook, context and perspective changed as well.* The shift meant that their goal was no longer an empowering and inspirational driver; it was now one that could be compromised and even trigger counterproductive behaviour. This can easily happen to all of us. The interesting question is, 'Whose fault was this – the lions or the King?' The leadership style of the King was not exactly encouraging and 'hands-on' but then again the lions were not engaged in fixing the problem but rather accommodating it.

As mentioned previously human behaviour is not random because we either act to gain something or to avoid something. These are our goals and they command our focus, influence our choices and drive our behaviour. If goals are carefully considered and thought through then they can wisely influence our

approach, options and tactics in a way that secures success. The quality of your goals directly influences the quality of your achievements. Consider some of the following 'alternative' goals that the lions could have adopted and especially note the behaviours that they would have provoked. Their goal could have been…
- To be always 'one step ahead' of our food sources in terms of strategies and tactics.
- To hunt in creative ways and carefully monitor the outlooks and activities of our food sources.
- To continuously improve the efficiency and effectiveness of our hunting teams.

Such 'drivers' as these would have triggered very different outlooks, approaches and activities. They would have involved a continual reassessment of current techniques and therefore tactics would have evolved at a much quicker pace; insight into the tactics of the zebras would have been gained. This could have triggered teamwork and alignment of purpose. It would have taken inspirational leadership however to have triggered this, perhaps not the King's strong point.

It is important not to confuse a strong and powerful personality with strong and powerful leadership. We all know of tyrants who have the authority to 'make' people do what they want them to and exercise this in a loud, aggressive and forceful manner. This is not strong leadership in most situations. In an emergency it might be totally appropriate however most times it is not. The wise approach is to create capability, build confidence and collaborate closely. If you reward curiosity and innovation it is easier to grow leaders. Any leader can create followers; exceptional leaders create other leaders.

Useful 'thought-provokers' about goals

Are your team's goals validated? Do you have a mechanism to sense check the things that are driving your team? Has 'drift' taken place in what people are focussed on? Is their attention on the next step or the final destination, or both?

Are decisions being made to make progress or to meet someone's approval?

Do you see instances in your organisation when the 'indicators of success' are being changed rather than the 'ways of working'? Often this is about looking for the easiest or most logical approach to a long-term problem or a case of treating the symptoms and not the root cause of it.

Jonathan Frost

7

THE FOURTH RESPONSE - INNOVATION

... "If things have changed, then you had better change too!" he roared at them. With the words of the King ringing in their furry ears the lions went away crestfallen. They discussed the situation at length, pooled their ideas and developed some different tactics.

At last the lions moved from 'reaction' to 'considered response' and this was triggered by an act of leadership from the King. Whilst his roaring about "You had better change too!" would not have won him 'Nice Guy of the Year' award it was a wise approach; this was no time for self-indulgent 'pity parties' because the Pride was in crisis and the hard work was not delivering results. I do come across people who are somewhat bewildered that their hard work and effort is not appreciated just because it did not achieve what it was meant to. I do understand their disappointment however 'effort' is not what your employer or customer is buying; they are not buying your time, they are buying what you can achieve in that time. They do not pay for your attendance at the workplace; they pay for your ability to influence people, situations and results whilst you are there. They are not buying your experience; they are buying what you can achieve because of that experience. That means if they are not getting the expected return from their investment in you, they will start thinking about their options. Only in Primary school do you get a medal for simply participating; in the real world of work you get your rewards based on what you actually achieve. Medals are strictly for achievers in the commercial environment.

In the workplace I would like to suggest that the following formula be used to ensure that a wise and consistent approach is taken when evaluating performance…

$$P=(A+R)i$$
Performance = (Activities + Results) x intentions

How we actually define good performance is very important to individuals and organisations because it creates context, drives behaviour and communicates corporate values; it directly influences what people do. If there is ambiguity in this area it seldom works well and usually ends up in an unhelpful compromise. The formula above captures the three important elements of performance; what people actually *do*, the *results* that they get and the *intention* or reason behind it all.

The direct link between 'activity' and 'performance' is blindingly obvious but we must differentiate between helpful, neutral and unhelpful activity. It is easy for us to think in terms of 'good' or 'bad' and this is unhelpful in two ways; a) there is a 'neutral' to consider i.e. behaviour that has no impact at all and b) it is better to talk in terms of helpful or unhelpful rather than right or wrong. This concept of neutral behaviour or activities is very important because it gives an 'illusion of influence' when in actual fact there is no influence. When people say, "I don't mind which approach we take" they are not backing any of the options and this is no help. It means that they have no 'ownership' for the success of an option and they can comfortably position themselves as observers or as pundits as things unfold. A player, captain or manager in the game cannot be neutral; they need to be proactively positive.

Point b) relates to the fact that thinking in terms of 'right' or 'wrong' can be very limiting because in the real world such judgements are not relevant and may not even exist. One choice of action might not be the smartest move, but at least it was taken with the right intention and it is too harsh to say it is 'wrong'. For the lions to change the zebra budget would not have been absolutely wrong, but it would not have been a wise move. It would have been more 'unhelpful' than 'wrong'. If we take the harsh judgemental factor of 'right or wrong' or 'pass or fail' out of the equation and look for ever more 'helpful' ways forward then we take the risk of failure out of it. This assists the development of creative options.

Individuals might be highly active and working very hard without it being good performance. The activity of the lions in chasing motorbikes across the plains of the Serengeti could easily be described as 'working very hard' and those that were engaged in it were certainly active. They had the blisters, the exhaustion and the sweat to prove just how hard they were working. It could not be considered as good performance however because it was not getting the results that were needed or specified. The lions could have applied a different strategy and poisoned all the grass in the grazing areas so that the zebras dropped dead during the afternoon. This would have enabled the hunting parties to bring back hundreds of extra zebras to the pride. This too could not be considered good performance because the lions would also have died after eating the poisoned meat. The importance of the *'intention'* in the formula becomes clear here. *The intention, reasoning or motivation behind any activity or results is a pivotal element of good performance.* Had the lions used the poisoning tactic their poor intention would have been revealed i.e. do what it takes to avoid the wrath of the King. Another unhelpful intention was to renegotiate the zebra budget; it was at total odds with the values of the Pride to be dominant, self-supporting and to care for each other because their numbers and health is their strength and competitive advantage.

So we know that good performance needs the right mix of activities, results and intentions and this can easily be seen in the workplace. Organisational and individual performance cannot just be all about the 'results' that are gained because that can create a whole load of unintended consequences. In retail there is a saying that goes *"Turnover covers over a multitude of sins"* and what this means is that as long as your sales are very high, nobody is going to lift the carpet and look for what might not be going so well. The halo effect of your sales figures will blind people to inefficiency, low productivity and inappropriate ways of working because there is sufficient excess to make these things relatively insignificant. The problem with this is that those 'other' things hidden under the carpet, which are avoiding inspection, may be pivotal. They might include areas such as wisdom, integrity and values; the short-term gain may create long-term losses. By way of an example almost every organisation in Europe, if not the Western world, has been severely impacted by the 'good performance' of the Banking sector in previous years. This highly rewarded 'good performance' focused all attention on achieving targets and it transpired that commonsense, wisdom, fairness, integrity and business acumen went flying out of the window. Staggeringly poor choices and incomprehensible actions were taken to achieve this 'success' which had the knock on effect in 2008 of bringing many banks and entire countries to the point of financial ruin. This 'success', according to performance targets, was rewarded within some Banks and was encouraged by them until the very end. *It is essential to recognise that good results can never be the sole indicator of good performance.* You and your team need to be doing the right things and doing them right! This is about engaging in tasks and initiatives that are wise, efficient, productive and well focused so that they create success. It is worthwhile asking those very questions of each other...

- What we are doing…*is it wise?'*
- 'What we are using up our energy on…*is it efficient?'*
- 'What we are spending much of our time on…*is it productive?'*
- *'Is what we do linked to our immediate, short-term and long-term goals?'*

So we see that getting the right results is not necessarily an indicator of good performance; an awareness and focus on *how* the results are being achieved is also needed. Good performance is as much about what you are doing as the results that you have. Back to the retail example, it is easy to double sales if you halve your prices; this action would achieve the goal, but it would also destroy the company. It is for this reason that individual, team and organisational *performance* has to be managed as opposed to just the figures being managed. In a very real sense it follows therefore that people need to have absolute clarity about their role and what is expected of them in their application of it. This would include an overall 'role statement' that explains in a few words the very rationale for that specific function; it would also need a list of the key activities that the person would be expected to undertake. This does not take away any freedom of initiative, all it does is clarify and capture exactly what is expected. This is then further added to by a very clear definition of what success looks like for each of the key activities and this serves as a benchmark and driver for individual focus, effort and activities. In this way we create a strong link between activity and results. Despite the fact that the lions were working very hard and had instituted around the clock hunting parties, it could not really be considered good performance because it was not delivering the 'indicator of success' i.e. a well fed Pride. As we saw earlier the situation needed much more than hard work; it needed innovation and change.

Change is at the very heart of improvement - if things stay the same as they are then they are not improving. Whilst this apparently suited the lions in our story it did not meet with the aspirations of the zebras and so they engaged in innovative thinking and audacious action. Their commitment, work rate and energy actually changed the whole Serengeti status quo and it forced change on the lions. Innovative thinking is that which identifies very different approaches, original perspectives, creative ideas and agile thought processes; it provides those who engage in it with a significantly competitive advantage.

It is widely held that people are generally resistant to change and I cannot accept this; I see it as a 'truism illusion' that has survived and replicated simply because it superficially resonates with people; it has not been seriously questioned. People do not mind winning the national lottery, receiving a salary increase, moving to a better house, getting a nicer office, being promoted, new hairstyles, new hobbies etc. all of which represent change. Children have a remarkable ability to adapt to new situations and circumstances and take 'change' within their stride. When watching a group of children at play in a 'Wendy house' you will see them constantly changing the rules, context and relationships as they go along and they mostly adapt and get on with the new game or scenario. It is when things do not evolve and change that they get bored and fractious; then the 'fallouts' occur. This so called resistance to change (if it does exist) appears to be learned behaviour rather than natural.

What we really mean is that people are resistant to change that they do not want. If change is not thought about, considered carefully and thought through then it represents the 'unknown', it is probably this that people are resistant to because it represents a risk or a threat. The more that change is honestly, openly and frankly talked about and discussed, the less resistance there is. The risk can be replaced by logic, curiosity, helpful imagination and balanced judgement. This is what the lions engaged in eventually, but only because they had to.

In the following chapters I introduce a helpful model that identifies the five stages required to implement long lasting and successful change. The King and the rest of the pride could have used these well, they include…

Awareness
Engagement
Activity
Consistency
Continuous Improvement

It has been my observation that these stages are valid for people at all levels and can seldom be skipped. It is possible to go through some of them almost instantaneously or simultaneously, but this does not apply to all. It starts off with the assertion that *change is a process*; it is not just an activity or a decision. Quite often I come across groups, teams and organisations which are surprised that things have not changed when the decision to was made and communicated and they ask "What more could we do?" Well quite a lot actually, let's look at this in the next chapters covering all five stages.

Useful 'thought-provokers' about performance

Is your team focused on changing things or maintaining things? Either focus could be correct as it depends on the situation. As a rule of thumb however if you are in maintenance mode and your competitors are not, you are going to end up with a disadvantage.

What is the reaction, in your organisation, to innovative thinking? Is this something that key influencers are reluctant to do or is it encouraged? Would people at all levels agree with you?

When was the last time that your team gained a significant win because of its innovative thinking? Does this happen often? Do the team feel extra proud when it does? Is it celebrated?

In your organisation are the management seen as the 'accelerator' or the 'brakes' regarding change? This is an important thought provoker because it is hard for you to judge and the answer could materially affect the outlook and approach of individuals. You could always do a confidential survey to find out.

PART 2

THE 5 STAGES OF CHANGE

Jonathan Frost

8

STEP 1 - AWARENESS

Awareness
Engagement
Activity
Consistency
Continuous Improvement

The role of a leader or manager is to deliver results in a wise and appropriate way. This involves influencing people, situations and results so that the team or organisation can achieve what it set out to do. To trigger a change in organisational performance you usually have to trigger a change in the individual performance of key people (including yourself) and to do this you have to provoke people to see things differently so that they decide to do things differently. This may be a change in outlook, approach, activities or mindsets and it usually involves helping people recalibrate their role, their contribution and the activities that they engage in.

Opportunities and Needs

The very first step to triggering personal change is to ensure that they are aware of either the *opportunity* or the *requirement* to change; as we have learned from the lions in our story this awareness is not a 'given'. Another word that could be used to describe this awareness could be 'alertness' which is all about being in a state of watchfulness i.e. having the ability to see and notice things that could have an impact on you. When the animals in the Serengeti come to a watering hole they are incredibly watchful, aware and alert. They face real dangers and are vulnerable as they come to the water and kneel down to it. They begin to narrow down their options to flee, they cannot run ahead because of the water and the left or right might be crowded. They are very exposed to attack from behind without the ability to leap away. They visually sweep the environment, their ears are attuned to the sounds of a bigger animal running and they approach very slowly; primed for instant flight. Attack could also come from the water. They are alert to any tiny thing that could represent a danger to them. When the lions come to the waterhole you do not see their alertness to the same level; there is an understanding that the threats to them are limited and they can be more relaxed. It is hard to be very relaxed and very alert at the same time; they each seem a hindrance to the other and if you think about it this does make perfect sense.

It is common for awareness and alertness to be seen as a mechanism for coping with danger and whilst this is true; it is not restricted to it. It is also a very powerful mechanism for identifying great opportunities. In the working world the time for action may be very short or the clues for the opportunity may be small and well hidden in the detail; this means that leaders and managers need to be in a continual 'state' of awareness.

Awareness of something simply means that it has entered your consciousness i.e. you have a realisation or recognition of it. It is not necessarily the same as having knowledge of it because you can be aware of something without fully appreciating what it means, why it exists or the ramifications of it. You can be aware of a strange sound getting louder, you know it is getting closer but you don't know anything else. This would trigger a real state of alertness. Another example might involve you driving your car and you notice a red light flashing on your dashboard. You don't know what it means but you are aware that something is not right; you become very alert to the feel of the driving wheel, you listen intently to the sound of the engine and you notice every vibration or shake. This example reinforces the important point that awareness is good, but not enough. The first step to initiating change with people is making them aware of either the opportunity or requirement to change but you also need the other four stages as well.

There are different types of awareness and they include *situational*, *numerical*, *people* and *business acumen* amongst others. Some people are very capable at reading situations accurately and fully. They have the ability to note events and happenings and link them together to see a process, picture or message. Such people are great assets to have on your team because they are able to give you insight into a situation so that you can make appropriate choices and take wise stances. Whilst this *situational awareness* comes naturally for some it is definitely a learned behaviour for all and the more that it is practised the easier and more fluent it becomes. As we discussed earlier it is all about concentrating your focus so that you actually 'notice' that which you see. Those that can see columns of figures and then extract meaning from them demonstrate *numerical awareness*. Some people can read a spreadsheet the same way that you and I can read a book and they make out the main themes and come to helpful conclusions. Again they are helpful people to have on your team because they can convert data into meaning so that meaning can be further converted into wise action. *People awareness* is all about being able to relate to, have rapport with and understand people. Again you will find that for some people this comes more naturally and they have the ability to intuitively tune-in to people and recognise their approach, outlook and meaning. Others have *business awareness* and they are finely tuned into business issues and are aware of the changes in their market, industry or customers; they might also have a great awareness of the practicalities of the organisational structure and culture.

Perhaps the most helpful characteristic of the very aware is an innate and strong sense of curiosity. Such people always convert an observation into a question, which is usually 'why, what or how'. They want to understand more and see how things link together. They are good at linking different elements to see patterns and relationships. For the aware, a 'cause' must be identified for every 'effect' that they notice; the 'cause-effect' principle is a driver for them, helping them to make sense of their world. It is my observation that this curiosity and helpful questioning actually creates mental energy rather than being a tiresome activity – *you never get tired when you are fascinated*.

As I mentioned before, for some people the different types of awareness are easy but for the rest of us there are helpful things that you can do to develop it; they are all about *focus*. Focus is a wonderfully rich word that we should use and apply more often. It talks about intensity; a converging that brings clarity, strength and impact. When you focus your binoculars you bring the subject from afar right into the centre of your vision and consciousness and you are able to see it in a much better light, detail and context. There are different ways that we can visually focus on things and they include using a hand to shield out the sun, squinting our eyes to narrow peripheral vision, moving closer to an object, using glasses to make it clearer, using binoculars to make it closer and using a microscope to magnify it. These are ways that we filter out peripheral things and filter in the things that we want to engage with. In a room full of people we filter out all the noise and chatter so that we can listen to (focus on) one specific conversation or sound. If we are concerned that a spider has crawled onto our leg we focus all our attention on that one particular area, highly alert for any sensation of movement or pain. So we see that we use 'focus' everyday and all day in our personal world and it makes sense to do it in our working world as well. This involves focusing on helpful things. There are at least nine useful areas of focus that will assist you to develop awareness and they include giving attention to...

Situations
Perspectives
Opportunities
Threats

Risks
Outlooks
Approaches
Patterns of Behaviour
Messages

It is very wise to strive for *situational awareness*. A situation is basically a set of circumstances, events or activities that combine together to create an impact. A business might find itself in a position in which its relationship with its biggest customer has deteriorated and has become a significant risk. This particular 'situation' has come about because of a chain of events including; one missed call, an incorrect assumption made during the manufacturing process, a distracted employee receiving the first query call, a defensiveness within the manufacturing team, an aggressive outburst from the sales director, a blame culture within the business and a lack of clarity about whose role it is to fix the problem. To make things really interesting both sales and manufacturing are fighting over which budget will take 'the hit' for the costs to fix it all.

All of these things combine together to create a situation. Awareness is all about making the effort to note the different elements of it and then piece them together to develop a helpful overall picture. As discussed earlier we know that the situational awareness of the lions was poor because they were not noticing the facts that they were seeing. Quite recently they may have seen less and less zebras, there may have been strange mechanical noises coming from the zebra quarter, they might have noticed a larger number of delivery trucks, they might have felt a 'sense of expectation' in the animal kingdom. Had they been attuned they would have heard the chatter and the commentary from the spectators of the situation.

If they had focused on *perspective awareness* the lions may well have seen more. This involves identifying the 'key influencers' in a situation and then spending some time looking at things from their perspective. When decisions are made or actions taken that significantly influence others, it is always wise to ensure that you thoroughly understand things from the perspective of stakeholders in your action. Had the lions thought about things from the King's perspective they would have understood his pressures, responsibility and approach and perhaps reacted much quicker. Had they understood the situation from the zebra's perspective they would have expected innovation from them and would have noticed some of the signs. Had they looked at the situation through the eyes of the parents of hungry lion cubs they might have understood the reality and urgency of the situation. Looking at things from different perspectives certainly gives a richer understanding and insight; the good news is that it is not difficult to do and is simply a matter of choosing to do it.

Opportunities are the chances that you have; a specific time or set of circumstances that will really help you to win or do something that you want to. Quite often they are fleeting and result from a momentary alignment of situations or happenings. If you relate this to the manufacturing example used earlier, this represents a significant opportunity for the competitors of the company that is having the customer relationship breakdown. If company B (competitor) is aware of the breakdown, the inconvenience this is causing the customer and their realisation that they should not be so reliant on one supplier – this could be great news for company B. There is a temporary window of opportunity for them and they need to react quickly whilst company A is distracted by their own ways of working. If company B has a stated goal of winning this customer, it is going to be much easier if they are aware of the opportunities.

An *awareness of opportunities* is a valued and important capability. It is not an easy thing to have and to achieve it you will find it is essential to have clear goals, targets and intended achievements in mind. The reason for this is that you have to link something that you see to what you want to achieve; when you make such a link you might just be seeing an opportunity! This is a self-priming process in that you are making your brain alert to the goal so that it can see other things in the context of it. You see conversations in the context of what you want to achieve rather than in their own isolated independent context. This allows you to make the necessary links and an opportunity is spotted. You see data, interactions, messages etc. through the prism of your goals and you therefore extract more value from them. This process seems to be about creating the right circumstances to 'filter in' some of the information available to you that you would not have done had you not primed yourself. If you are thinking of buying a certain car of a certain colour, you will suddenly start seeing a lot more of them around. The number of them has not really changed;

it is just that you are now noticing the ones that are there – you primed yourself to do this. I am sure that you can see how powerful a practice this is if you choose to prime yourself to see opportunities. The same principle applies to *awareness of threats* in that you notice the situations, issues and activities that pose a threat to you because you are seeing those things in the context of your goals. We see the importance of goal-focused behaviour for the leader because it is the key to recognising opportunities and threats.

Awareness of risks is similar to threats and they are synonyms of each other however I find it useful to define them slightly differently. I see threats to success as being quite a macro, bigger picture issue that tend to happen and which you don't necessarily create them yourself. The threats exist and you have to be aware of them and make decisions accordingly; an example might be the presence of a large competitor in your region or pending legislation that could influence your business practice. The weather can be a threat to a retailer; if you sell very warm fleecy jackets and it looks like it will be a very mild winter then you have a threat to your business. You might not be able to do anything about the weather, or the legislation or even the large competitor directly i.e. you cannot remove the threat but you can manage the risks associated to it. *Threats create risks* and wise managers are aware of the threats to their operation and they manage the associated risks caused by them. You can manage the risk of lost custom to the competitor by engaging in more marketing, diversifying your range or creating a superior customer experience. You can manage the risks of the legislation by being agile with your business model and building flexibility into your investments and service development. The risks to turnover that come from the weather threat might be managed by choosing a different channel in a different area to sell through and buying different stock which is more appropriate. The risks could create strategic opportunities as you identify wise ways of managing them. Of course this is only possible if you are aware of the risks. The value of this approach is wide as well as deep and can even apply to individuals as they build their careers; being aware of opportunities, threats, risks and situations can be very helpful indeed.

Awareness of outlooks is linked to the awareness of perspectives type thinking in that it is very helpful to understand the outlook (one element of perspective) of the different people who are stakeholders in your success. Outlook is the viewpoint that people have on life, their standpoint, their angle, their frame of reference and it is a very significant factor in how they see things and feel about them; and therefore a significant influence on their behaviour. The better insight that you have into someone's outlook, the greater the opportunity you have to influence him or her and gain a helpful rapport. It should be noted that people might not be aware of their own outlook because it is not something that we spend time thinking about unless provoked to do so. There are a multitude of different outlooks in life and they include having a positive, negative, optimistic, persecuted, religious, logical, practical or carefree outlook. The *approach* that somebody chooses to take can be greatly influenced by outlook but not necessarily so; they could have years of training that compel them to take a certain approach or the organisational culture within which they work may dictate certain approaches. This is why it is important to develop an *awareness of approaches*.

We tend to be repetitive in terms of how we act and react in situations or when going about our daily activities and this provides us with the opportunity to focus on other things and become aware of them; rather than having to consciously think about everything we do. It is obvious that we all develop our own processes, systems and ways of working that suit us and help us to function. We slip into what I call 'patterns of behaviour' and it is very useful to identify these in your key stakeholders. If you notice their typical ways of responding to things, making decisions, investigating, verifying or managing people; then you will notice that patterns emerge and this knowledge and insight represents an opportunity to understand and influence them. All of the above enables us to extract meaningful messages from the behaviours and activities of others.

When you are trying to influence people the first step is to make them aware of the opportunity or the requirement to change. Your level of awareness about them will significantly assist your success in this. It is very important to note however that this awareness is just conscious knowledge; it is not a decision to change and no change has actually taken place. Just because somebody is aware that it is needed does not mean that they have engaged in it. Every smoker is aware of the deadly results of the habit but this awareness does not influence many to stop. They need to *engage* in change and that topic is covered in the next chapter.

Useful 'thought-provokers' about awareness

Are your team clear who they need to influence more (or differently) to enable success? Are they aware of the opportunities to influence key influencers?

On a scale of 1-10 how would you rate your team on their levels of awareness of opportunities, threats and risks? Do you have mechanisms that provoke you to 'take time out' to think about these, identify them and build them into your thinking?

Do you think that your team has the right balance between being 'alert and aware' with being 'comfortable and relaxed'? This is about having a helpful situational awareness so that the team can act, react and respond appropriately to the happenings in their organisational life.

9

STEP 2 - ENGAGEMENT

Awareness
Engagement
Activity
Consistency
Continuous Improvement

The second step to helping people to develop new skills and capability is to ensure that they are personally *engaged* in it. This goes beyond knowing about it…it becomes 'knowing it personally'. It is when a general point becomes a personal discovery to you that compels you to action. Engagement is all about a depth of involvement or committed participation; it reflects a 'captured' focus and attention. When a couple become engaged it demonstrates an intense commitment to and involvement with each other. In the same way to be engaged in an opportunity or activity also reflects a significant commitment and involvement that goes beyond a day-to-day approach.

Engagement is usually triggered when you have an awareness of something and you note that it reflects either an opportunity to gain something or a need to avoid it. This need for a response provokes you to consider the whole situation in more depth and from different perspectives. Imagine that you are in an unfamiliar building, it is pitch dark, late at night and you hear a high-pitched scream; you quickly move from awareness of a sound to engagement in the ramifications of it. You start thinking about 'who', 'what', 'why' and your mind races for answers as you consider the ramifications for you. What should you personally do in response? Should you run? Should you investigate? Should you dial for emergency services?

The move from awareness to engagement is basically a function of 'richness of thought'; it happens when the individual carefully considers what they have become aware of and then makes a decision to do something about it. Let's apply this to the situations that we referred to in the previous chapter; you may remember that for one organisation there was a threat of impending legislation that would affect their ability to carry out 'business as usual'. Awareness of this triggers thoughts and makes links and this provokes you to carefully consider the ramifications; you start to see the risks that your business faces. You moved from awareness to engagement when you started identifying the *specific ramifications* to your business and when you started thinking of *appropriate activities* that you could do in response. You are no longer an observer of the situation, you have engaged with it in order to influence an outcome. The same applies to the business that has a large competitor present in their region. It is just a fact or a data point that this other company exists and awareness of it alone will not shape strategy or influence performance in any way. You have moved from an awareness of a situation to an engagement with it when you start identifying the risks and commence thinking what you can do to mitigate them, including what you can do differently in order to compete with them.

It is not a 'given' that awareness (step 1) automatically becomes engagement (step 2). We see that the lions were aware of the change of tactics from the zebras but they were simply observers of it at first, they did not really engage with the situation. It seemed to take a dose of anger from the King and a large portion of humiliation to trigger their engagement in a solution. For the lions this situation was both a real opportunity for them as well as a significant threat. It was an opportunity (that they missed) to be seen as real leaders and cunning heroes because if they had reported back to the King with the news that zebras had discovered motorbikes and then followed up with, "But leave it with us, we will solve this problem!" they would have been seen as true leaders. It was a threat to them because the change of zebra tactics significantly eroded their contribution and performance; unfortunately they had to have the pain of being roared-at and humiliated before they fully engaged. Roaring and shouting of course is not the recommended way of helping people to discover wiser approaches because it is both unreasonable and counterproductive. This approach simply generates obedience and subservience when what you really want is purpose driven leaders working wisely on their own initiative.

The recommended way of inspiring engagement is to help people to think more deeply and differently about things so that they can discover salient facts and be moved to do something about them. One of the most common and effective ways of doing this is to ask relevant open questions. We all know about the power of asking questions that begin with who, what, why, when and how because they cannot be shrugged off with one word responses; they make you think about it enough to be able to answer it appropriately. By way of an example I have found the following questions most useful when coaching people…

"What does this situation mean to you…"

"How are you personally impacted by…?"

"For you…what is an acceptable outcome and what is the ideal outcome?"

"What are the costs and what are the benefits of this approach?"

Such questions trigger the individual to ponder. One of the more endearing things about the human brain is that it seems incapable of hearing a question without looking for an answer. *Do you agree?* (Did you notice that you momentarily stopped and answered the question in your mind?). This human need to answer questions is a very useful tool to use when you are trying to engage people.

Consider the following question; *"How would you explain the colour turquoise to a man born blind?"* It is a difficult question and at first you may try to avoid it however you will come back to it and consider it. At first you may compare the colours to temperature and talk about it being cool or warm…and quickly realise that this has no meaning to the individual. After that you are pretty stumped. My point is that this question has really got you thinking.

"What is the difference between *curiosity* and *engagement*?" This is an interesting question because mild curiosity can easily masquerade as engagement when in actual fact it is simply a game that people play or a habit they follow. It is engagement when the individual has a purpose to the questions other than entertainment; it is when they are linking their questions and your answers in order to gain or avoid something. Curiosity often leads to engagement but they are not the same. The relevance is that a curious person may ask many pertinent questions and be fully 'in the know'…but not at all 'in the game'. This is demonstrated in what I call the *illusion of engagement* and this happens when individuals appear to be thoroughly interested in what you are saying or explaining and they nod vigorously and ask a wide range of relevant questions. Often these are about the practicalities of doing and implementing what you are talking about. It is just an illusion of engagement however because they have a totally different reason for their questions and attentive listening. Their mission is to prove that you *should not* in fact be going down this road and they are earnestly seeking out reasons for not doing it. They have decided *in advance* that they don't really want to do this and are engaged in the search for ammunition to validate their decision. This is not to be confused with the person who is very engaged and her pragmatic approach compels her to understand the challenges more fully. The concrete proof that it is actually an illusion and it does not reflect real engagement becomes very clear over time; no activity takes place. It is talked about, discussed and debated however it never results in new ways of working.

Engagement is a significant step forward but it

certainly is not enough. Remember that it is still just a mental state and no change in activity or practice has actually taken place. A change of mind may have occurred and is welcomed but this is not the same as a change in behaviour or tactics. Obviously a change of approach or position is evidence of engagement however it should be understood that the longer the time gap between 'engagement' and 'new activity' the higher the risk that change will not take place. In essence engagement changes the way that people see and feel about things and we know that this can influence what they do.

Useful 'thought-provokers' about engagement

Are your team just aware of the mission or are they actually engaged in it? The difference between these two will be seen in a proactive approach and the demonstration of ownership. When awareness has transferred to engagement it creates a sense of ownership. It triggers a keenness to discuss it and keep the issue 'on the radar'. You will find that your team raises issues with you; they need only to be guided and steered as opposed to pushed and directed.

Are enough open type questions used in your meetings and discussion? Sometimes we prefer to avoid situations in which the team don't know the answers to questions or are discussing issues where there is ambiguity or controversy. I would strongly urge you to value the concept of team discovery so that you can provoke thought, discussion and debate, it is through this that creative and innovative solutions are developed.

10

STEP 3 - ACTIVITY

Awareness
Engagement
Activity
Consistency
Continuous Improvement

Trigger, Recognise & Reward

The third step to influencing people is to trigger, recognise and reward smart activity. It is about inspiring people to actually do things, to expend their energy in a way that impacts people and situations. This is what work actually is: 'an activity involving physical or mental effort to have an effect and get a result'. It is the conclusive proof that the individual has fully engaged in the change and it is the first stage where things start being done differently, better or quicker. This takes things out of the theoretical and firmly places them into the arena of the 'real' and 'practical'.

At this point in time it is wise to applaud *effort and compliance*, it is not the time to be pointing out all the shortcomings or better ways of doing it; it is the time to be reinforcing the effort. When leading, managing and influencing people it is vitally important to be aware of and focus on 'progress' not just success.

Progress is a win!

In a football game if a team scores a goal in the first ten minutes all of their supporters go wild and applause and cheer. They do not sit stony faced and say, "We had better wait for the final whistle before cheering, we have not won yet!" – they excitedly celebrate the great progress that their team has made. Progress should always be looked for and celebrated because it means that change is taking place, that we are closer to our goals and that we are doing some good things! It would have been silly for Usain Bolt's parents to watch him running at the age of 5 and say "You are no where near to being the fastest runner in the world!" or "I know hundreds of people who can run faster than you". They would rather have marvelled at his 'situational' capability, noted his progress and fed it back to him positively; this would have encouraged him. His progress would have made him stand out and made it obvious that his was a future worth investing in. To have not noticed his progress and to focus only on what he had not yet achieved would have been damaging for a young boy. It would have recalibrated his progress to be a failure and it would have made him feel that nothing was ever good enough. When children feel this way they often give up because they do not see a direct link between their effort and the praise that they receive; it is the same in the world of work. If the link is not obvious it is a leadership failing that needs to be addressed urgently. It can create an environment in which the focus is on avoiding the risk of failure as opposed to being excited about the risk of success. Any fool can criticise; it takes a 'real' leader or manager to trigger, notice and applaud progress. It takes real leaders to inspire people to reach their full potential. 'Activity' a very crucial stage of change. Leadership can be hard work, appear thankless, create risks and be time consuming; this is one of the reasons that 'being at the top' can be quite lonely. Everybody needs encouragement and praise without being patronised. Coaching, discussions, thought provoking and group activities are good for reinforcing the progress. Quite often I meet leaders who allegedly do not have the time to engage their key people in 1:1 meetings, wide ranging chats or focused discussions. Their interactions are governed by metrics and 'results'. This cuts off opportunities to recognise progress and to inspire, enthuse and reward.

This is the stage when individuals start to do things differently and do different things. The old adage tells us that if we do what we always do, then we will get what we have always got; the logic is flawless and it resonates with our experience. This is not about getting people to just work harder like the lions did initially, a search is needed to identify better ways of doing things. You might have to do the same things however you can always look for different ways of doing them. This might be about refining your technique so that the investment of your energy or resources provides a helpful increase in productivity. It might be about looking at the systems and processes and finding ways that you can be more efficient. You may need to review the quality of output from a very objective standpoint so that you add significant value to your contribution. Sometimes it is about helping people to recalibrate their role so that energy and focus is placed in more appropriate pursuits and activities.

The above improvements are about doing what you currently do but better; you also need to think about doing some different things as well. Instead of adjusting and amending what you do you might have to go right back to the drawing board and innovate new ways. The lions had never blockaded a petrol station before so this was a new activity for them, an approach developed through their discussion about how to change. If they had not decided to do something new then they would still be running after motorbikes.

As a leader you have to trigger people to act in helpful ways and do things that enable the organisation to meet its goals. You have to inspire those in your sphere of influence to take action so that they can contribute to the organisation's success. Whilst you have the authority to direct or instruct them to do something, this is not the wisest approach because it creates compliance rather than commitment. Obedience to your commands may help in the very immediate term but over time it creates a dependency on your leadership and this dampens initiative and proactivity. It will then mean that you have to own more of the processes and get even more involved in the detail; this is not consistent with your leadership role. Whilst you are doing the job that somebody else really should be doing...who is doing yours? If your line manager has to do parts of your job to fill the void then you may find that the assumption is made that you are not able to cope in a leadership role or that you have reached your career summit. Neither of these is true of course but it is a logical conclusion to draw.

A manager's focus needs to be on enabling their team and helping them to step up. It involves assisting with their development to do their job well and reach their full potential. Quite often I see that the development activities, improvement plans and training registers often have a focus on helping an individual to be ready for their *next* step-up role, to help them be promoted. Whilst I see the wisdom of this I do have a concern that there appears to be no expectation of a 'standard of excellence' in their current role. Are they OK, good or excellent in their current role? Advancement is only appropriate if they have excelled at their current role i.e. they are experts doing what they currently need to do in a wise, innovative and highly productive way. It makes sense to invest in them to be a role model in their current position before focusing on the next one. To do this you want to influence their choices, options and decisions about how they go about their work.

One of the more successful ways of making sure that your team feels a sense of ownership for their tasks and activities is to sell, persuade or convince them of the appropriateness of a specific strategy, approach or set of actions. It is more powerful to guide, suggest and inspire people than to simply instruct them because it develops commitment and ownership. 'Sell' is the right word to use because when you are exercising leadership and provoking someone to discover better ways of doing things; you want them to 'buy' into your thinking and tactics so that they personally own them. You never want to hear the phrase "Your plan did not work" because you want the person responsible for delivering it to actually own it! I have outlined below a useful system that you can use to persuade, convince and sell better ways of working to your team. I call it the 'retail analogy'. Retail companies are *driven by the need to provoke you into action* and in their particular case that is a two fold process and it involves persuading you to a) make a decision to buy and b) exchange your money for the retail products. This process has been going on for thousands of years and the principles behind it are really useful when you are looking to influence people. You are in fact persuading them to see a need to make a decision and then you are triggering them to make it and act on it. Let us look at this in a bit more detail.

The first step for a retailer is to create a helpful environment, one that promotes their products in the best possible light and which exposes the many choices available to you. I call this 'silent selling' and it includes window displays, promotional banners, in-store signage, posters, point of sale literature and attractive displays; these all work together to attract your attention and create a demand for action (purchase). In the same way leaders and managers need to create the most engaging and helpful working environment; one that accurately captures the bigger picture, creates a focus on the overall goals, shows the many options, promotes good choices and makes it easy and interesting to engage with. This is not about decorations or fancy coffee machines it is about an emotional and intellectual environment that inspires energy, focus and positivity. There is an old saying that goes 'It is hard to soar like an eagle when you spend your time surrounded by turkeys!' and I certainly know what this means. You have to create the environment that stimulates, informs and challenges people. It needs to empower individuals and groups to wisely take massive action. This is the result of strong leadership with individuals who focus further than authority, routines and processes; they have a focus on identifying and nurturing talent. Think about the environment that your people experience on a day-to-day basis at work. Are they inspired to peak performance because of it or despite it? It is not the physical elements of the workplace that I am talking about; it is the impact on people's outlook and perspective. Do the meetings, 1:1 discussions, briefings, informal chats and other interactions stimulate enthusiasm or dampen it?

The second retail step is for their staff to approach you; they do this so that they can influence you to buy. Wise sales people watch to see if you are a 'bored', a 'browser' or a 'buyer' so that they can make the most helpful approach. They know the bored are simply there to pass time and hope that as they wander around, the retail environment is attractive enough to switch them to be browsers. You may well have the 'bored' in your workplace and this is why it is important to have the right and helpful environment i.e. one that clearly displays the route to success and the value of the journey. They figuratively wander around seeing everything but are not really moved by it, until they see an element that they can relate to and engage in. You may have to approach them to stimulate some 'internal demand' for involvement. The behaviour of shopper 'browsers' is quite different to the bored because they have a much more defined focus in their activity; this focus may be on a range, brand or a particular product function. Often they are evaluating the different options and are actually looking for reasons to buy. In the workplace we have the browsers too and we should value them and see them as an opportunity rather than a frustrating problem. We want to take the browsers, those at the sidelines of full engagement, and help them to find an approach that will work best for them. We want to approach them and influence them to buy. The art of retail is about attracting customers, converting them into browsers and then converting them into buyers. The art of influencing individuals and teams is very similar and also involves matching possibilities, plans and goals to people and then helping them to decide to 'buy' into them and engage with them.

The third stage that retailers use in their selling process is 'establishing needs'. Experience has taught them that the things that interest shoppers might not actually be the right solution for them at all; what somebody wants is not necessarily the same as what they actually need. They talk to customers asking helpful questions to gain insight and then use their product knowledge to either reinforce what the customer is thinking or to propose alternatives. This requires a helpful interaction and the same applies to the workplace. Individuals need to be engaged with; their thinking, aspirations and perspective need to be understood so that they can be aligned to the whole team and organisation. In order to influence them you need to understand them and the better the quantity and quality of interactions, the easier this is.

The fourth stage of the retail selling process involves 'presenting products'. Having engaged with you the retailer has established a helpful rapport and has understood what you need and want; they now present to you products that they think are ideal. Essentially they now sell to you and do this by noting the 'features' of the items and then talk about the 'benefits' of owning them. This is a good model to follow when we are looking to 'sell' a new approach, a different outlook or smarter tactics. The better we explain the features of what we are saying so that they understand it, the better they are able to digest what we are saying and evaluate options. When we are very clear about the benefits of the approach it becomes a 'buying point' for them. It would be wise not to assume that they understand what you are saying or that they intuitively 'get' the benefits of it. If these things are talked through in a way specifically focused to them, then you have a great opportunity to make the sale i.e. to influence them. It is my experience that everybody, at some time, pretends that they understand what is being said and nod their heads knowingly to communicate this when in reality they are lost! We all do this at times and hope that subsequent data will fill in the blanks. A well-implemented 'features and benefits' presentation avoids this.

The fifth stage of the retail selling process is the 'close'. This is when they move on from presenting information and benefits and directly encourage the customer to buy. This direct encouragement can take many forms and they vary by their directness. The 'direct close' does what is says on the tin and the sales person simply asks 'Do you want to buy it?' The 'alternative close' is a little subtler and is my preferred favourite. It provokes you to make a choice between two options rather than a yes/no decision. 'Do you want the red one or the blue one?' assumes that you are taking one or the other and is very successful. The 'summary close' simply recaps all the benefits, starting with the least impactful and culminating with the 'killer sales point'. The individual then goes quiet and waits for the customer to say yes. I do not see these as manipulative in any way; they are simply ways of encouraging a customer to buy…and to buy today if possible. This is an important principle for leaders and managers as well because when selling ideas, strategies, different ways of working you need to 'close' the sale and ask for a direct commitment to do it. It is generally accepted that most people don't actually like being sold to; they prefer to 'buy' things on their own terms. This happens in the workplace as well when you are looking to influence the team, they want to discover better ways as opposed to being told to do them. In the world of sales nobody takes offence when objections are raised to the sales pitch; in fact they are welcomed because they reveal areas in which the potential customer is 'unsold' so they have another opportunity to persuade them. In the same way it is wise to welcome 'push back' or 'resistance' to change because it simply means that they are not seeing it the way you do – they are unsold.

So we see that the third stage of influencing change is all about activity. Having become 'aware' of the opportunity or requirement they have become 'engaged' and this has lead to new 'activity'. It is at this stage that the tips, hints and techniques that you have coached begin to be used. This is the stage that shows how strong your influence has been on their outlooks, approach and thinking. Change is definitely starting to take place and it impacts on more than just the individual that you are focusing on. Their sphere of influence becomes impacted and this can change situations and results.

Useful 'thought-provokers' about activity

Do you celebrate progress? Remember back to the story; the lions enjoyed the running much more than the zebras because the 'pursuit of gain is always a lot more fun than the fleeing of pain'. Winning is always more fun than 'not losing' and you can use the concept of 'celebrating progress' to inspire, reward and motivate people. This helps momentum to be established in the shortest possible time.

Do you lead an ongoing pursuit for improved quality, productivity and efficiency? I call this the *'QPE focus'* and it is all about betterment. If you keep this on everyone's agenda you will be delighted what your team discover and how they will encourage and compete with each other for the best improvement. This is a necessary initiative otherwise the team will simply revert to working harder and this may not be enough.

How do your team describe your leadership style? Do you tend to be more instructive and directive or do you prefer to suggest, advise and sell ways to improve things? It is very hard for you to really see your own management style and so it would be profitable for you to have some informal chats with people that you can trust; ask them to talk objectively and frankly about your style. I am not suggesting that you try to have a popular approach because that might not be situationally appropriate; you do however want to have the most helpful approach.

11

STEP 4 - CONSISTENCY

Awareness
Engagement
Activity
Consistency
Continuous Improvement

In your efforts to help people to achieve their full potential you have made them aware of the opportunity to be better. You have triggered an engagement within them that has resulted in their trying out new approaches and activities. Changes in behaviour have taken place and you now want to help them to absorb and adopt the new ways into their standard ways. This may involve them changing the things they do or adding to the things that they do. The next stage of change that you want people to discover is called 'consistency'. It is about doing things the same way over time so that you can comfortably expect and predict that they will achieve the outcomes that you are looking for.

Let's go back to our football analogy. You are the manager of a team and there is an important game coming up; you are thinking about team selection. Player A is a natural genius with amazing flair but an unpredictable temperament. In one game this season he scored a hat trick, in another he punched an opponent and was sent off. Last week, from out of nowhere, he pulled off a spectacular winning goal, in the last 5 minutes of the game, kicking the ball from within his own half; the fans love him. The week before he had a stand up argument, on the pitch, with the captain and walked off before the end. This shook the team and the game was lost. Player B does not score quite as many goals as player A and they are never spectacular; however he seldom misses when an opportunity is provided. He is never going to win 'goal of the year' award but every year he is within the top three goal scorers at the club. You really need to win the game this coming Saturday and you cannot field both players. Who are you going to choose, player A or player B? I would go for player B because I value consistently good performance higher than variable brilliant/poor performance.

This thought-provoker applies to the workplace. Sometimes people rely on flashes of genius and the pulling of proverbial rabbits out of proverbial hats. These streaks of genius are to be welcomed but not relied on. I want to suggest the value of consistency in performance and whilst this is not as big and glitzy as feats of magic, in the long run it delivers consistent results. Inconsistent performance delivers inconsistent results. In the workplace if the ways of working are consistent then it enables a kind of helpful comfort and certainty. When things are consistent people can relax and spend their time focusing on specific areas because they can enjoy situational awareness rather than heightened alertness. This is a very important stage of our 5 stages of change; *it is when the new behaviour, thinking or approach becomes the new standard way of doing things.*

This consistency should come easily because, as mentioned earlier, humans tend to be creatures of habit. Much of our behaviour has a regular tendency and by this I mean that we like having our preferred ways and customs of doing things and establishing a personal 'norm'. This enables us to act without having to think too hard and this in turn leaves our 'thinking' energy to spend on more interesting or taxing things. We develop habits through this repetition and in the absence of other stimuli they become adopted and need a good reason to change; they can be hard 'self imposed rules' to break.

It should be noted that we develop our own habits and they can be positive, neutral or negative; all three are just as easy to develop. Consider this question…when you get in your car do you put the key in the ignition and then put on the safety belt or do you do it the other way around? It makes no real difference at all and I am sure that you can easily justify your approach. The point I am making is that you will consistently do it one way or the other. This is a 'neutral habit'. If you scan your rear view mirror and side mirrors very frequently when you are driving then you have developed a very 'positive/helpful habit'. If you cross your hands over a few times when steering your car you have apparently developed a bad/unhelpful habit.

We see habits developing all the time at work and you can use this for the good of yourself, your team and your organisation. As mentioned in an earlier chapter it is probably more appropriate to change this thinking to 'helpful', 'neutral' or 'unhelpful' habits as a means of removing the 'value judgement' of good or bad. It is definitely helpful to provoke people to identify as many of their work habits as possible because it gives them the power to change them if they see a need or opportunity. Perhaps a better way to describe these consistent ways of working is to apply the phrase I used earlier in the book i.e. 'patterns of behaviour'. Of course this can be an uncomfortable activity for some and it needs to be done wisely. The good news is that developing a helpful habit takes no longer than it does to develop an unhelpful habit – it is simply a matter of repetition. Habits are formed when we repeat doing things to the extent that we no longer think about them, they are simply absorbed into our 'internal programming'. They cease being a conscious choice or decision and become a 'response to a stimuli'. This means it is well worth spending a few minutes reflecting on the habits that you have in your working world…

- What do you do without thinking?
- Where does your leadership 'autopilot' take you?
- How effective, efficient and productive are your habits?
- Do you habitually plan for OK, Good or Exceptional outcomes?

We know that habits are formed to help us to operate effectively however that does not mean that they always develop helpfully and therefore need to be inspected every now and again. We could habitually strive for 'good' because we are not yet in the habit of striving for 'excellent'.

The goal of the 'consistency' stage is to embed the different outlooks, thinking, activities etc. that you have triggered into new 'habitual' ways of doing things. Again recognition, encouragement and rewards need to be given to those travelling on this journey of change. People will value your support as they attempt to bring about change in their 'ways of working'. This is certainly a good time for celebrating progress. At this stage of the change process the responsibility for success is clearly shifting from you onto them. They have been made aware, engagement has been inspired and new ways of working have been applied. This is about people 'owning' the new and different outlooks, approaches and activities as opposed to simply 'renting' them for a short while. Another way of saying this is that there is a need for these new ways to be 'adopted' as opposed to 'tried'. Adoption implies an ongoing strong commitment to the ways; this will always yield good results.

Useful 'thought-provokers' about consistency

As a leader, what are your helpful habits at work and what would you say are your unhelpful habits? Areas to consider in this question include things like performance chats with the team, 1:1 meetings, coaching etc.

Which does your organisation value the most; is it the spectacular stars or the consistent deliverers? It is important that consistency is valued because it creates consistent results. Very often the 'stars' have the capability to deliver consistent results rather than outstanding flashes of brilliance; they just need reassurance that it is valued.

Has the responsibility for 'betterment' been transferred? Are you still driving the changes you want to see or are you now 'nudging the tiller' and just guiding and assisting people as they continue the journey of self-improvement?

12

STEP 5 - CONTINUOUS IMPROVEMENT

Awareness
Engagement
Activity
Consistency
Continuous Improvement

The final of the five stages of influencing change is 'continuous improvement'. This is about continuously and consciously achieving incremental improvements so that over time significant further progress is made. You have an important role as a leader to keep this focus alive and to give as much encouragement, praise and reward as you can. Having journeyed through awareness, engagement, activity and consistency your team members will have developed new approaches, ways of working and ways of thinking. They have achieved new and helpful habits. This might have moved them from 'Ok' to 'Good' or from 'Good' to 'Very Good'; now the challenge is to continue the journey and move to 'Excellent'. This is a bit of a 'solo flight' for your team members because the awareness of further opportunities to improve is mainly self-generating and self-fulfilling.

Once 'consistency' is beginning to take hold, it is good to markedly shift the emphasis from 'compliance' onto a 'quality' focus. It is a good thing that people are actually doing things differently and better; now the challenge is to see just how good they can be. The 'coaching' expertise of leaders and managers yields great dividends at this stage. *Coaching is the process of engaging with an individual or a team to help them discover better ways of 'seeing' things, 'feeling' about things and 'doing' things.* Lets look at this statement in more detail. It is about 'helping' people; this is far removed from just pointing out what they are doing wrong and it is certainly not about 'being on their case'! The emphasis is on provoking them to *'discover'* better ways. What you 'discover' you own. That knowledge and deep understanding resides in your own brain and it is immediately and continuously accessible. This new awareness and enlightenment is not in a book; it does not need the explanation of someone else. Being directly relevant and personal to you it is fully applicable to your circumstances. I am hoping that you have had some 'light bulb' moments as you read this book and that you discovered some principles or options that bring clarity and technique to your leadership role. When such discoveries are owned they can be transferred to other areas of life and the lessons are cumulative and they build up into capability. When this capability is wisely and frequently applied it becomes a recognised expertise. The 'experience' that is gained from this discovery, capability and expertise is vital to both you and the organisation that you work for and it becomes quite a marketable asset of yours.

99% of our learning does not take place in a lecture hall

Discovery is all about finding things, coming across them or locating them. It implies much more than simply gaining new information; it infers a positive and powerful experience of something being uncovered or unearthed. It rightly implies richness to what is available to be discovered. It is my view that discovery is nature's routine learning method. Observe the children of today engaging with new technology without pause, concern or hesitation. They never read manuals they simply 'dive in' and learn by doing – they discover ways of getting the best results. Do you remember, as a child, attending 'bike riding academy'? That lecture on 'how to maintain balance by sticking out your opposite leg' if you felt you were falling over? No? Well neither do I because we did not have such lectures or training. Mum and Dad coached us as we wobbled along! We learned about balance, speed and direction as we raced around. We discovered how to use our energy wisely and how to alter our approaches when encountering gradients. Our experiences taught us the wisdom of caution and the effects of momentum. We did not have classes; we had *experiences* and we discovered good, solid and reliable principles from these. I am obviously very positive and committed to training activities, books and development resources but my point is that discovery through experience is a tremendous enabler. *Leaders, managers and key influencers can radically change capability (in themselves and others) through coaching and the creation of learning experiences.*

It is important to note however that all experiences are not necessarily learning experiences. My point is that it is not so much the actual experience that we learn from; it is what we do with it, how we think about it and what learning we extract from it. If we do not spend time reviewing it and looking for learning points then it is just an experience and not a 'learning experience'. The coaching process is essential in helping people and teams to discover better ways of doing things. If your role in the organisation is to deliver results through the work of others, then you need to deliver inspirational and instructive discovery-based coaching. This involves coaching chats, discussions and formal sessions to help them to discover all the lessons from their experiences. *Your role is to convert day-to-day work into a powerful and enabling learning experience.*

The '3 Review Questions'

A powerful but simple coaching activity that you can immediately use to create learning experiences is the '3 Review Questions' model. This technique triggers a coaching interaction that prompts the continuous improvement process. If your team expect these questions to be asked then it will helpfully influence their outlooks and ways of working. The questions are…

What worked well?
What did not work so well?
What would you do differently next time?

The reason for starting off with *'What worked well?'* is because it provides an opportunity to reinforce good practice, helpful activities and admirable efforts. This tends to be more motivating and it enables the chat to commence. It is too easy for conversations to become an uncomfortable discussion about what went wrong as opposed to what could have been better and this hinders engagement in discovery; it can convert a useful learning experience into a risk. Use this first question as an elevator to raise the level of conversation and to provoke thought. See it as the first in a three-stage process, don't allow it to simply be an introduction to 'what went wrong?' You never know in advance which of the three questions is going to yield the most productive learning; if you really knew the answers in advance you would not need to ask the questions! It should not be taken for granted that someone actually knows what he or she did well to generate such a good result. This is important because if somebody does not know what created their success, they cannot replicate it next time. It also creates an obvious and relevant opportunity for praise.

Recognising what someone has done well earns you the right to point out what they have not done well; it is this activity that separates the 'fair' manager from the 'critical' manager. At first people can be a bit hesitant to look at 'what worked well' because they do not want to appear boastful or arrogant. You may have to help the conversation initially by asking about the wide range of factors that contributed to the situation or by asking about it from different perspectives. It is also important that people do not jump to conclusions about this because it could mean that they focus attention on unhelpful areas and this could be a distraction. If someone is convinced that their sales growth is due to 'discounted prices' it could lead to a real focus on cost and price-cutting...when in actual fact the real issue was the quality problems of a competitor. You have to persevere with the first question; people tend to find it easier to notice and talk about the 'not so good' - remember you may be trying to get them to discover something that they have seen but not noticed. Some useful questions to ask that will help keep the focus on 'what worked well?' include...

- 'What were the signs that things were going well?'
- 'At what point were you sure that you had really been understood?'
- 'It sounds as if they had some very tough questions...what helped you or enabled you to have such good answers?'
- 'What do you think made that difference? Why do you think they relaxed at that point?'
- 'You feel the discussion started well...what do you think they were thinking at that point?'

I chose my words carefully when asking the second question; *'What did not work so well?'* It is intended to comfortably and honestly talk-through things without getting critical or apportioning blame. If this question is not asked carefully it can provoke a 'blame game' that is little use to anyone. The issue is not about 'who is at fault?' we are just trying to understand why it did not go the way we wanted it to so that we can extract learning points. There may be a wide variety of reasons and we have to look at all the options and consider everything. This cannot happen if someone feels that they need to talk defensively. In coaching sessions people often rephrase this question to *'what did I do wrong?'* or some other negative phrase. I usually intervene to correct it because it changes the whole tone of the discovery. It is not about 'right' or 'wrong'; it is about 'what would be more helpful'.

You may find that you have to keep bringing people back to the original question because we are looking for understanding, not solutions. It is easy for people to jump onto talking about what they would do differently without learning why it happened that way in the first place. The fuller the discussion about what did not go so well, the more interesting and relevant are the learning points that emerge. It is also important to avoid the trap of looking for 'the' problem as opposed to a range of contributory factors causing an issue.

The third question asks, *'What would you do differently next time?'* It is a vital question that should still be asked even if things went brilliantly. You want to learn from every experience and then prepare for continued or even improved results. If things did not go according to plan it is essential to recognise what we could have done differently so that we can do this next time! Again this is far from being critical. The best way of achieving a good result with the '3 Review Questions' is to be curious about answers and the reasons behind them. Position yourself so that it is you who are looking for answers to these important questions; it is not you asking others to explain themselves. Continual use of such 'thought provokers' is very good for a team. Imagine the benefits to the organisation if everybody consistently asked the '3 Review Questions' of themselves and each other. Imagine if it were to become standard practice in the company! I maintain that they are, by themselves, powerful enough to create a learning and 'continuous improvement' culture.

So the overall goal of this 5-step discovery process is to identify changes that you would like to influence and then engage with individuals to guide them, over time, through the different stages. I have provided a few examples below about how this might work and how you can use the process. It covers three fictitious members of my team - Matt, Anna and Bruce.

MATT: I have noted that he needs to exert a firmer leadership style, to be more assertive and to be more focused on meeting deadlines.
Awareness - YES
Engagement - YES
Activity - YES
Consistency - NO
Continuous Improvement - NO

He is aware of the opportunity and has started doing things differently - this is proof of his engagement. He has not developed any new 'habits' yet and it is only happening when he consciously thinks about it. This is going to be the focus of my 1:1s and coaching chats with him. I am looking for opportunities to praise his progress and provoke thought about other things he can do. Matt is fully engaged and actively changing things; that is why he is at stage 3.

ANNA: I have noted that she needs to focus on increasing her accuracy and attention to detail. She is glossing over details and missing significant things.
Awareness - YES
Engagement - YES
Activity - YES
Consistency - YES
Continuous Improvement - YES

Anna is fully aware and engaged; she has successfully worked hard to address this issue. She has developed a few personal techniques to pay closer attention and 'filter-in' important things and has even addressed some procedural issues to reduce the risks. I am delighted with this progress and when we chat about it during 1:1s and coaching conversations I am encouraging her to build on this success. She has engaged one of her direct reports in the same thinking and this is beginning to show results.

Anna is fully engaged and has taken action. She has then added further improvement and expanded the influence of it; that is why she is at stage 5.

BRUCE: I have noted that personally, he delivers great results however he is limiting success to what he personally can do. He needs to focus on taking his large team with him. Currently he operates like a 'one-man-band' when in reality he needs to 'conduct his orchestra'.
Awareness - YES
Engagement - YES
Activity - NO
Consistency - NO

Continuous Improvement - NO

Bruce is not finding this easy. He is aware of the issue and he agrees with it but cannot really see what to do about it. I have issued him some thought provokers and I have found a case study of someone who Bruce really respects having the same issue early on in his career (I have given this to him). During my 1:1 with him I am going to talk about the case study and ask for his observations, thoughts and ideas. I will be helping him to discover some specific tips, hints and techniques and agreeing with him what to adopt, and when we will again discuss progress.

Bruce is aware and engaged but at this point in time he has not discovered appropriate actions to take; that is why he is at stage 2.

You can see how the application of the 5-step process does not create limitations; it actually encourages and liberates ideas because it provokes you to think. It helps you to provide practical and directly relevant coaching, support and advice.

Useful 'thought-provokers' about continuously improving

As a leader, what stage are you at (1-5) in terms of your ability to influence people, situations and results? Are you engaged and active in 'betterment'? What would your 'proof of progress' be for this?

Can you identify a list of helpful 'experiences' that you can provide for your team members as a way of assisting their development? This might involve them attending specific meetings for development, engaging in projects, leading particular initiatives etc.

What are the areas for 'continuous improvement' that you personally should be focussing on? Consider this in terms of your skills, knowledge, experience and outlooks.

Jonathan Frost

12

SUMMARY OF MODELS AND TECHNIQUES

This book has been written primarily for you who are leaders, managers and key-influencers because your success depends very much on the performance of others and you need practical and proven techniques to influence those people. It has provided a wide range of tips, models and techniques that you can use to influence people and in turn this will impact on situations and results. It started with a parable about change and progressed onto the 5-stage process for changing outlooks, approaches and activities. In this final chapter I provide a summary of the different models presented to make it easier for you to refer to them.

PART 1

The Zebra Analogy

In Chapter 1 we started looking at the Zebra Analogy and recognised the risks of taking comfort in a 'natural order'. It was clear that 'competitive advantage' is not a 'right' and that it will always be temporary. We noticed that the lions were using their observations about life in the Serengeti to reinforce their 'worldview' as opposed to constructing it. We saw the dangers of having a culture of 'passive resistance' rather than one that promotes and inspires 'active curiosity'; it stopped the lions from seeing the changes.

In Chapters 2 & 3 we noted that 'different thinking' could be a real game changer. We also recognised that it is possible to have good vision even with poor eyesight. When we looked in detail about what made the difference for the zebras we noted that their advantage was in actually having a) A Vision and b) Meaningful Communication. It was these two attributes that gave the zebras the advantage and the lack of them that made the lions vulnerable. Without this strong collaboration and meaningful communication the whole herd would not have been able to grasp the concept of the vision, own the journey or personally make a difference.

The 'Football Analogy' was introduced provoking thought about the differences in engagement and contribution between the spectators, pundits, the manager, the captain and the players. It provoked you to be sure of which role you are meant to be playing.

In Chapter 4 the initial response of the lions to the change was revealed; it basically involved doing nothing. We noted a number of reasons why this might be the response to the change that the zebras initiated. They included...

- Lack of awareness – not linking data together
- Preference to cope rather than to change
- Denial
- Not knowing what to do
- It is worth you looking for these symptoms in your organisation.

In Chapter 5 we saw the folly of trying to outrun motorbikes. 'Work More, Work Harder' was the second response of the lions and whilst this can be very appropriate in the short term; it creates problems if applied in the long term. We saw that there were 5 risks associated to this strategy…
- Treating symptoms and not root causes
- Extra becomes the 'new norm'
- Focus shifts from winning to coping
- Creation of leadership voids
- 'One level down' working

There are occasions when difficulties and challenges require more *inspiration* than *perspiration* and trying to outrun a motorbike was a fine example of this.

In Chapter 6 we saw the third response to change and it involved trying to redefine success. It is often wrong in the face of failure to try to change 'standards of performance' before really trying to change the current tactics to achieve them. We looked at the difference between reacting to change and responding to it. The difference is more than just an issue of timing i.e. reacting is much quicker; it is more about engagement and the quality of thinking that is being applied. When you 'consider' all of the options and carefully choose which one to take you are 'responding'. When you simply do what feels right then you are just reacting. Both are appropriate tactics to take depending on the circumstance you are facing; it is important however to make this a conscious choice.

In Chapter 7 we saw the lions begin to innovate and then turn things around. A formula to describe good performance was introduced.

$$P=(A+R)i$$
Performance = (Activities + Results) x intentions

It was noted that performance is only to be defined as good if the right activities are being undertaken, with the right intentions; which result in the preferred outcomes. It was also noted that change is at the very heart of any betterment; if things are staying the same they cannot be improving.

PART 2

From Chapter 8 onwards you were introduced to a proven model that can be used to instigate, manage and lead change in your organisation.

5 Stages of Change Model

Awareness – there is an awareness of the need or the opportunity to change.
Engagement – there is a personal involvement in change.

Activity – smart activity that represents change is triggered, recognised and rewarded.

Consistency – the new behaviour, thinking or approach is now the 'standard' way of doing things.

Continuous Improvement – includes continuously and consciously achieving incremental improvements over time.

Chapter 8 explains the first stage i.e. 'Awareness' and highlights that you should be looking for situations that 'require' change as well as those that would 'benefit' from it. The lesson from the lions is that we should always be looking for change and sometimes it is a response to a threat and at other times it is taking advantage of an opportunity. It was asserted that the role of a leader is to influence people, situations and results and to do this you need to create awareness of the opportunities and requirements. This chapter noted some different types of awareness as follows...

Situational awareness: the result of extracting meaning from circumstances, events or activities that collectively make an impact.

Perspective awareness: the result of seeing situations from many different perspectives (especially those of the key influencers) and creating a rich understanding by linking them together.

Opportunity and *Threat* awareness: the result of having a clear focus on things that influence the achievement of goals.

Outlook awareness: the result of tuning into and understanding the outlooks (perspective, standpoint, angle) of your key influencers.

'Patterns of behaviour' awareness: the result of noticing the repetitive ways of thinking, working and interacting of others.

The key is to use this awareness and to enable it in others in order to influence their behaviour, approach and ways of working.

In Chapter 9 we focused on engagement and confirmed the need to convert awareness into engagement. The key methodology for this is to provoke people to think more deeply so that they 'discover' a personal perspective and generate a personal desire to get involved. Open Questions (who, what, why, when, how and which) are very useful tools to achieve this.

In Chapter 10 we saw the first real sign of tangible change i.e. Activity. This is about helping people to do different things; or do things differently. In this chapter the concept of 'Trigger, Recognise and Reward' was introduced. The importance of focusing on and rewarding progress was highlighted as a means of stimulating more helpful activity; it was reinforced that progress is actually a win. The 'Retail Selling' model was presented as a powerful means of influencing people and this included…

Silent Selling
The Approach
Establishing Needs
Presenting Products
Closing the Sale

Chapter 11 introduced Stage 4 – 'Consistency'. This was all about helping people to develop new, helpful and powerful habits. This involves converting the 'new' ways into the 'standard' way. It talked about the benefits of consistency including the ability to operate in an environment of 'awareness' rather than 'alertness'.

Chapter 12 was all about 'Continuous Improvement' and it noted that this is the stage where the responsibility for progress and the continuation of the journey rests with the individual. As a leader you have created the right environment and provided assistance to help them to move through the different stages – it is now time for them to 'fly solo'. The responsibility is theirs to make continual incremental improvements and the responsibility is yours to coach them in this. We talked about coaching being a process of helping people to discover better ways of doing things and that this is vital because 99% of our learning takes place at work. The '3 Review Questions' were introduced as a powerful coaching tool…

What worked well?

What did not work so well?

What would you do differently next time?

It happened on a Friday morning...

"On the plains of the Serengeti in Africa the sun comes up, the animals stir and little zebras stretch and yawn. Everyone starts preparing for the challenges of the day. They have to find good grazing spots and good water supplies. More importantly they have to be prepared to run...and run very fast.

They know that to survive they need to run faster than the fastest lion. This is because across the plains, the lions are also waking up and they are preparing for the challenges of their day. The lions know that if they are going to survive they have to run; at least to run faster than the slowest zebra. Whether you are a zebra or a lion it is guaranteed to be a challenging and active day.

It was on a Friday morning however that the 'natural order' of things changed once again. Only half of the hunting party reported back to the King of the pride...and they had no kills at all.

Outraged at this the King roared his disapproval and asked for an explanation.

"The zebras beat us up!" was the reply, "We could not defend ourselves. They stampeded us, so did the elephants and then the baboons threw rocks at us".

The King stared at his hunting party speechless.

"They have told us to leave the Serengeti…or else!" wailed the leader of the hunt."

Jonathan Frost